Southern Living.

# The SOUTHERN HERITAGE COOKBOOK LIBRARY

# The SOUTHERN HERITAGE
# Beef, Veal & Lamb
## COOKBOOK

**OXMOOR HOUSE**
Birmingham, Alabama

**Southern Living.**

## The Southern Heritage Cookbook Library

Copyright 1984 by Oxmoor House, Inc.
Book Division of Southern Progress Corporation
P.O. Box 2262, Birmingham, Alabama 35201

*Southern Living*® is a federally registered trademark belonging to
Southern Living, Inc.

Library of Congress Catalog Number: 83-61838
ISBN: 0-8487-0608-0

Manufactured in the United States of America

### The Southern Heritage BEEF, VEAL & LAMB Cookbook

*Manager, Editorial Projects*: Ann H. Harvey
Southern Living® *Foods Editor*: Jean W. Liles
*Production Editor*: Joan E. Denman
*Foods Editor*: Katherine M. Eakin
*Director, Test Kitchen*: Laura N. Nestelroad
*Test Kitchen Home Economists*: Pattie B. Booker, Kay E. Clarke,
    Marilyn Hannan, Elizabeth J. Taliaferro
*Production Manager*: Jerry R. Higdon
*Copy Editor*: Melinda E. West
*Editorial Assistants*: Mary Ann Laurens, Karen P. Traccarella
*Food Photographer*: Jim Bathie
*Food Stylist*: Sara Jane Ball
*Layout Designer*: Christian von Rosenvinge
*Mechanical Artist*: Faith Nance
*Research Editor*: Janice Randall
*Research Assistant*: Evelyn deFrees

#### Special Consultants

*Art Director:* Irwin Glusker
*Heritage Consultant:* Meryle Evans
*Foods Writer:* Lillian B. Marshall
*Food and Recipe Consultants:* Marilyn Wyrick Ingram,
    Audrey P. Stehle

*Cover (clockwise from front):* Old-Fashioned Beef Stew (page 54),
Crown Roast of Lamb with Fruit Dressing (page 85), and Veal Birds
(page 74). Photograph by Jim Bathie.

# CONTENTS

Introduction                    7

Beef                            9

Veal                           59

Lamb                           82

Variety Meats                 107

Sauces  &  Gravies            123

Good to Know                  132

Acknowledgments    138      Index    140

# INTRODUCTION

Modern steak lovers may cringe to read recipes for stewing steak or cutting beef for broiling a fraction of an inch thick. But before we condemn our ancestors as boors, let's look at the reasons for such sacrilege. Of the cows, sheep, and pigs brought from England, only the pigs could thrive under the circumstances in which they found themselves. Pigs, turned loose on the "mast," not only survived but went on to fame as Virginia hams. But the flesh of cows and lamb, prey to predators and unable to forage successfully, was so stringy and dry that it was barely fit for food until the mid-1700s.

Excavations of colonial trash deposits at Williamsburg have turned up bones of beef from calf to adult, and cattle bones found on the lower James River confirm a report published in England in 1649 that beef was raised there to victual ships. Still, Virginians imported tons of English beef, dried, salted, or pickled, in the 1700s. Governor Francis Fauquier ordered 700 pounds in 1768, the casks weighing up to 230 pounds each.

Beeves were frequently slaughtered as veal in order to use them before they reached tough maturity. In time, the quality of meat improved so that by 1745, Williamsburg butcher Benjamin Hanson was able to advertise "good Grass Mutton or Beef," some of which came from Shirley, Carter Burwell's plantation. Another butcher, Samuel Wilkins, furnished meat to the Duke of Gloucester Street tavern for over 20 years.

No part of a meat animal was wasted: old recipes abound for preparing tripe, haslet (liver), tongue, and ears; cowheel, calf's head, and udder were delicacies. All were served in the finest homes.

Mutton was eaten less regularly; townsmen had to keep their sheep near their homes because of wild animals. Like pork, mutton spoils rapidly, so farmers slaughtered only in cold weather. An exception was the headstrong William Byrd of Westover. In his diary (1709-1712), he told of enjoying roast mutton for two days in the midst of a Virginia July, but on the third day, "I ate no good dinner because our mutton was spoilt . . . however I ate some of it."

The intervening years have seen the development of quality meats our forebears rarely, if ever, tasted. And Americans are still, right after Argentinians, the world's most ravenous consumers of beef.

# BEEF

## Heartiest of Meats, A Feast of Choices

It would be unthinkable to stay for long in Texas without being a party to an authentic barbecue. Temptations to overeat seem to be endemic to the South, and Texans lay on the down-home hospitality so thick as to test the character of the hardiest trencherman. At a barbecue, expect to eat your weight in beef steaks and brisket, all juicy and dark with wood smoke.

There are still ranch women in Texas who can break down a 500-pound beef carcass as skillfully as a trained butcher. Prior to slaughtering, the animal, usually a yearling, is penned up and fed on corn for several weeks. This has a tenderizing effect on the meat that pleases everyone except the old-timer who doesn't think he's eating beef unless it has to be thinly sliced and savagely chewed.

Before the introduction of refrigeration and freezing equipment, beef that could not be eaten immediately was boiled and canned or put down in brine or packed in a saltpeter mixture for corning. Dried beef jerky has been current since the cowpoke used it to assuage his hunger without getting off his horse. Modern backpackers use a version of the Indians' nourishing trek snack, pemmican, which was jerky grated and mixed with fat and dried berries.

The beef industries of Central Florida and the Great Plains were built on the descendants of cattle originally brought in by the Spanish. Some Southern Indian tribes tended cattle and were forced to leave them behind when they migrated west. Settlers who came to stay on such vacated lands found scattered remnants of those herds running wild and, therefore, scarcely fit to eat.

Generations of scientific breeding and feeding have resulted in the fine beef we enjoy today. And Southerners know many ways to make the most of good beef. From tender steak broiled over white-hot coals to savory brisket moist-cooked and sauced, here are some of those ways.

*Steak at its best: Thick Texas Steaks (page 26) cut an inch thick and grilled outdoors. Rolled brisket (page 16) is cooked on the grill in a jacket of foil. For tenderness, slice diagonally across the grain.*

# ROAST VARIETIES

## BEEF TENDERLOIN WITH BORDELAISE SAUCE

1 (4- to 5-pound) beef
   tenderloin, trimmed
1 clove garlic, minced
Bordelaise Sauce

Rub tenderloin with garlic.
Place tenderloin on a rack in a
shallow roasting pan. Tuck narrow end under to make roast
more uniformly thick. Insert
meat thermometer, if desired.

Bake, uncovered, at 450° for
45 minutes or until meat thermometer registers 140° (rare).
Cut tenderloin into 1-inch-thick
slices, and arrange on heated
platter. Serve with Bordelaise
Sauce. Yield: 12 to 15 servings.

*Beef Tenderloin, decorated
with a tomato rose, is
luxury dining at its height.*

Bordelaise Sauce:

1  shallot, minced
1  slice onion (about ½-inch
   thick)
1  small carrot, scraped and
   cut in half lengthwise
6  whole peppercorns
1  whole clove
1  bay leaf
2  tablespoons all-purpose
   flour
2  cups beef broth
¼  teaspoon salt
⅛  teaspoon pepper
¼  cup plus 2 tablespoons red
   wine
1  tablespoon chopped fresh
   parsley

Combine all ingredients in a
medium saucepan. Cook over
low heat 15 minutes, stirring
occasionally. Remove peppercorns, clove, and bay leaf before
serving. Yield: about 2 cups.

Garnishing a fillet of
beef is the subject of
discussion in this
paragraph from an 1877
cookbook *Practical Cooking,
and Dinner Giving:* "Sometimes skewers are put in,
stuck through a turnip
carved into a cup, and this
cup holds horse-radish. But
some people say skewers re-
mind them of steamboat
cooking; then some people
are not easily pleased. . . .
Not that I am particularly ad-
vocating skewers, but I think
dishes *taste* better . . . when
they are decorated in almost
any manner. . . ."

*Lyndon B. Johnson roping a young horned Hereford on his Texas ranch, 1965.*

## TURN-OF-THE CENTURY FILLET OF BEEF

3 tablespoons butter or margarine, softened
1 (4- to 5-pound) beef tenderloin, trimmed
1 teaspoon salt
½ teaspoon pepper
Sherry-Mushroom Sauce

Preheat oven to 500°.

Rub butter over surface of tenderloin; sprinkle with salt and pepper. Place tenderloin on a lightly greased rack in a shallow roasting pan. Turn narrow end under to make roast more uniformly thick. Insert meat thermometer, if desired.

Place in oven, and immediately reduce temperature to 400°. Bake, uncovered, for 50 minutes or until meat thermometer registers 140° (rare).

Cut tenderloin into 1-inch-thick slices and arrange on a heated platter. Serve with Sherry-Mushroom Sauce. Yield: 12 to 15 servings.

*Note:* Tenderloin may be garnished with tomato roses.

Sherry-Mushroom Sauce:

1 tablespoon butter or margarine
1 tablespoon all-purpose flour
1 cup beef broth
½ pound fresh mushrooms, sliced
½ cup pale dry sherry
Salt and pepper to taste

Melt butter in a heavy saucepan over low heat; add flour, stirring until smooth. Cook over medium heat, stirring frequently, until browned. Gradually add beef broth; continue cooking, stirring constantly, until thickened and bubbly. Stir in remaining ingredients. Cook over low heat, stirring frequently, until mushrooms are tender. Yield: about 1½ cups.

## MRS. LYNDON B. JOHNSON'S FILLET OF BEEF

1 (4- to 5-pound) beef tenderloin, trimmed
14 to 16 slices bacon
½ pound fresh mushrooms
3 tablespoons butter or margarine
Fresh parsley sprigs (optional)

Place tenderloin on a rack in a shallow roasting pan. Turn narrow end under to make roast more uniformly thick. Wrap bacon slices around tenderloin to completely cover. Secure each slice with a wooden pick. Insert meat thermometer, if desired.

Bake, uncovered, at 400° for 35 minutes or until meat thermometer registers 140° (rare).

Clean mushrooms using a damp paper towel. Remove stems and reserve for use in another recipe. Sauté mushroom caps in butter over low heat 5 minutes.

Cut tenderloin into 1-inch-thick slices and arrange on a heated platter. Serve with sautéed mushrooms. Garnish with parsley, if desired. Yield: 12 to 15 servings.

Collection of Business Americana

*Mrs. Rorer presides over her cooking class, c.1902.*

## LUCIE COUNTY BEEF WELLINGTON

1 (5-pound) beef tenderloin, trimmed
1½ cups dry red wine
2 tablespoons lemon juice
1 tablespoon Worcestershire sauce
2 teaspoons pepper
1 teaspoon salt
Mushroom Pâté Filling
Pastry (recipe follows)
1 egg, beaten
1 teaspoon water

Cut tenderloin into bite-size pieces, and place in a large shallow dish. Combine wine, lemon juice, Worcestershire sauce, pepper, and salt. Pour mixture over meat; cover and marinate overnight in refrigerator, turning occasionally.

Prepare Mushroom Pâté Filling. Cover; refrigerate overnight.

Prepare pastry; cover and refrigerate overnight.

Drain meat; discard marinade. Combine meat and Mushroom Pâté Filling, stirring well; set aside.

Divide pastry into 12 equal portions. Roll each portion into an 8-inch circle on a lightly floured surface; reserve excess pastry. Spread each circle with 1 cup meat mixture. Fold pastry over filling, and pinch edges to seal. Place Wellingtons, seam side down, on lightly greased baking sheets.

Combine egg and water, mixing well; brush on each Wellington. Roll out excess pastry; cut into decorative shapes, and arrange on top of Wellingtons, if desired. Brush with remaining egg mixture. Bake at 375° for 30 minutes or until golden brown. Yield: 12 servings.

### Mushroom Pâté Filling:

1½ pounds fresh mushrooms, finely chopped
8 green onions, finely chopped
2 tablespoons butter or margarine
4 (2¾-ounce) cans French liver pâté
1 teaspoon salt
½ teaspoon pepper

Sauté mushrooms and green onion in butter in a medium skillet until tender. Stir in remaining ingredients, mixing well. Remove from heat; let cool completely. Yield: 1½ cups.

### Pastry:

5 cups all-purpose flour
1½ teaspoons salt
1⅔ cups shortening
¾ cup plus 1 tablespoon ice water

Combine flour and salt in a large mixing bowl; cut in shortening with a pastry blender until mixture resembles coarse meal. Sprinkle ice water evenly over surface; stir with a fork until dry ingredients are moistened. Shape dough into a ball. Yield: enough for 12 individual Wellingtons.

## STANDING RIB ROAST

1 (10-pound) standing rib roast
2 cloves garlic, minced
2 teaspoons salt
1 teaspoon pepper
2 tablespoons all-purpose flour

Rub roast with minced garlic, salt, and pepper. Sprinkle 2 tablespoons flour over entire surface of roast. Place roast, fat side up, on rack in a shallow roasting pan. Insert meat thermometer, if desired.

Bake, uncovered, at 450° for 1 hour. Turn oven off; leave oven door closed. Let roast stand in oven until desired degree of doneness: about 1½ hours or 140° (rare); about 2 hours or 160° (medium).

Transfer roast to a warm serving platter. Let stand 10 minutes before slicing. Yield: 8 to 10 servings.

*Note:* Roast may be garnished with tomato roses.

## NORTH CAROLINA PRIME RIB OF BEEF

1 (5-pound) standing rib roast
1 medium onion, thickly sliced
1 clove garlic, halved
1 teaspoon salt
½ teaspoon pepper
¼ teaspoon ground ginger

Rub roast with onion and garlic. Sprinkle with salt, pepper, and ginger. Place roast, fat side up, on rack in a shallow roasting pan. Insert meat thermometer, if desired.

Bake, uncovered, at 400° for 10 minutes; reduce temperature to 350°, and bake until desired degree of doneness: about 1 hour or 140° (rare); about 1½ hours or 160° (medium).

Transfer roast to a warm platter. Let stand 10 minutes before slicing. Yield: 4 to 6 servings.

*Note:* Roast may be garnished with tomato roses.

When George Washington Vanderbilt visited Asheville, North Carolina, he was smitten with a certain mountain view and envisioned a great house to focus on the scene. To realize his dream, he engaged architect Richard M. Hunt, and Biltmore House materialized in the 1890s. The enormous Banquet Hall captured the medieval spirit in detail, yet it contained practical items as well. The 1895 silver meat server (right) was designed to keep both meat and gravy warm during lengthy banquets.

## GREENBRIER ROAST SIRLOIN OF BEEF

1 (4-pound) boneless sirloin roast
2 tablespoons vegetable oil
1 tablespoon salt
1 tablespoon coarsely ground black pepper
1 tablespoon all-purpose flour
2 cups whipping cream
2 tablespoons Cognac

Brown roast on all sides in oil in a large skillet. Place roast, fat side down, on rack in a shallow roasting pan. Sprinkle with salt and pepper. Insert meat thermometer, if desired.

Bake, uncovered, at 375° until desired degree of doneness: about 1 hour or 140° (rare), about 1 hour and 10 minutes or 160° (medium).

Transfer roast to a warm platter; let stand 10 minutes before slicing. Reserve pan drippings.

Combine drippings and flour in a saucepan. Cook over medium heat, stirring constantly, until smooth. Gradually add whipping cream, stirring well. Set aside and keep warm.

Place Cognac in a small saucepan; heat just until warm. Ignite with a long match, and pour over roast. Slice roast and serve with sauce after flames die down. Yield: 6 to 8 servings.

Collection of Business Americana

## BOURBON RIB ROAST

2 tablespoons soy sauce
½ teaspoon salt
½ teaspoon pepper
1 (7-pound) standing rib roast
Basting sauce (recipe follows)
¼ cup bourbon

Preheat oven to 500°.

Combine soy sauce, salt, and pepper. Brush roast on all sides with soy sauce mixture. Place roast, fat side up, on rack in a shallow roasting pan. Insert meat thermometer, if desired.

Place roast in oven; reduce heat to 325°. Bake until desired degree of doneness: about 2 hours or 140° (rare); about 2½ hours or 160° (medium). Baste every 15 minutes with sauce.

Transfer roast to a warm ovenproof serving platter. Let stand 10 minutes.

Place bourbon in a small saucepan; heat just until warm. Ignite bourbon with a long match, and pour over roast. Present roast to guests while flaming. Slice and serve after flames die down. Yield: 6 to 8 servings.

### Basting Sauce:

¼ cup plus 2 tablespoons olive oil
1 tablespoon apple cider vinegar
1 tablespoon Worcestershire sauce
1 teaspoon pepper
6 dashes hot sauce

Combine all ingredients in a small bowl, stirring well. Yield: about ½ cup.

## ROAST BEEF WITH YORKSHIRE PUDDING

1 (9- to 10-pound) standing rib roast
Salt
Coarsely ground black pepper
Individual Yorkshire Puddings

Score roast in a diamond pattern, making cuts about ¼-inch deep in fat. Sprinkle roast with salt and pepper.

Place roast, fat side up, on a rack in a shallow roasting pan. Insert meat thermometer in roast, if desired.

Bake roast, uncovered, at 450° for 15 minutes; reduce heat to 300°, and continue baking until desired degree of doneness: about 2½ hours or 140° (rare); about 3½ hours or 160° (medium).

Transfer roast to a warm platter, reserving ¼ cup clear pan drippings for Individual Yorkshire Puddings. Let roast stand 20 minutes before slicing. Serve with Individual Yorkshire Puddings. Yield: 10 to 12 servings.

### Individual Yorkshire Puddings:

2 cups all-purpose flour
1 teaspoon salt
2 cups milk
4 eggs, beaten
¼ cup clear pan drippings

Combine flour and salt in a large mixing bowl. Combine milk and eggs, beating well; add to flour mixture, beating constantly with a wire whisk until batter is smooth.

Place twelve 6-ounce custard cups on a jellyroll pan. Spoon 1 teaspoon reserved drippings into each cup. Place jellyroll pan in a 425° oven for 5 minutes.

Pour about ⅓ cup batter into each cup. Bake at 425° for 15 minutes. Reduce heat to 350°; continue baking 15 minutes or until puffed and golden brown. Unmold to serve. Yield: 12 individual servings.

*Roast Beef served with Yorkshire Puddings.*

Courtesy of The Greenbrier

# GRILLED BRISKET

1 (4- to 4½-pound) beef
  brisket
2 tablespoons garlic salt
1 tablespoon coarsely ground
  black pepper
Panhandle Barbecue Sauce

Sprinkle brisket on all sides with garlic salt and pepper. Wrap in heavy aluminum foil, leaving a hole in top of foil. Place brisket on grill over low coals. Cover grill; open vent. Cook 2 hours and 15 minutes or until meat is very tender.

Transfer brisket to a warm platter; cut diagonally across the grain into thin slices. Serve with Panhandle Barbecue Sauce. Yield: 12 servings.

Panhandle Barbecue Sauce:

2 (14-ounce) bottles catsup
1 cup firmly packed brown
  sugar
½ cup butter or margarine
3 tablespoons lemon juice
2 tablespoons liquid smoke
2 tablespoons Worcestershire
  sauce

Combine all ingredients in a large saucepan, stirring well. Bring to a boil; reduce heat. Simmer, uncovered, 30 minutes, stirring occasionally. Yield: about 3½ cups.

# BARBECUED BRISKET OF BEEF

1 (3-pound) beef brisket
1 teaspoon salt
½ teaspoon pepper
Hot sauce to taste
  (optional)
2 cups water
3 medium onions, chopped
1 tablespoon shortening,
  melted
½ cup catsup
½ cup tomato soup
1 tablespoon lemon juice
1 tablespoon firmly packed
  brown sugar

Brown brisket on both sides in a large Dutch oven, browning fat side first. Add salt, pepper, hot sauce, if desired, and water. Cover and simmer 1 hour. Do not drain.

Sauté chopped onion in shortening in a large skillet until tender. Stir in catsup, tomato soup, lemon juice, and brown sugar, mixing well.

Pour mixture over brisket in Dutch oven. Cover and simmer an additional 1 hour and 15 minutes or until meat is very tender, stirring occasionally.

Transfer brisket to a warm platter; cut diagonally across the grain into thin slices. Serve with sauce remaining in Dutch oven. Yield: 8 to 10 servings.

# OVEN-BARBECUED BRISKET

1 (3-pound) beef brisket
2 tablespoons liquid
  smoke
2 tablespoons Worcestershire
  sauce
2 teaspoons celery seed
2 teaspoons pepper
1 teaspoon salt
1 teaspoon garlic salt
1 teaspoon onion salt
Barbecue Sauce

Place brisket, fat side up, in a shallow 2½-quart casserole. Combine remaining ingredients except Barbecue Sauce, mixing well. Pour mixture over brisket; cover and refrigerate overnight.

Place casserole in oven. Cover and bake at 250° for 5 hours.

Remove brisket from casserole; discard marinade. Cut brisket diagonally across the grain into thin slices.

Return sliced brisket to casserole; pour Barbecue Sauce over top. Bake, uncovered, at 300° for 30 minutes. Remove brisket to serving platter, and serve with Barbecue Sauce. Yield: 8 to 10 servings.

Barbecue Sauce:

2 cups water
⅔ cup catsup
½ cup red wine vinegar
¼ cup plus 2 tablespoons
  firmly packed dark
  brown sugar
2 teaspoons prepared
  mustard
2 tablespoons instant
  minced onion
1 teaspoon salt
½ teaspoon pepper
½ teaspoon paprika

Combine all ingredients in a large saucepan. Bring mixture to a boil; reduce heat and simmer, uncovered, 15 minutes, stirring occasionally. Yield: about 3 cups.

*Cowpokes playing cards are not easily stampeded. They knew the true merit of "Page Woven Wire Fence" back in the middle 1800s.*

DON'T STOP THE GAME, PAGE FENCE WILL STOP THEM.

Calvert Lith Co., Detroit.

## TEXAS PRIZE BRISKET OF BEEF

1 (4- to 5-pound) beef
  brisket
5 medium carrots, cut into
  2-inch pieces
2 medium onions, peeled
  and quartered
1 stalk celery, cut into
  2-inch pieces
1 bay leaf
1 teaspoon salt
¼ teaspoon pepper
4 cups water
Horseradish Sauce
Minced fresh parsley
  (optional)

Place brisket, carrots, onion, celery, bay leaf, salt, pepper, and water in a Dutch oven. Bring to a boil; reduce heat. Cover and simmer 3 hours or until meat is very tender.

Transfer brisket to a warm serving platter; discard broth. Cut brisket diagonally across grain into thin slices; pour Horseradish Sauce over top. Sprinkle with parsley, if desired. Yield: about 12 servings.

Horseradish Sauce:

1 large onion, finely
  chopped
¼ cup butter or margarine
2 tablespoons all-purpose
  flour
1 cup beef broth
1 (5-ounce) jar prepared
  horseradish
1 cup vinegar
½ cup sugar
2 whole cloves
2 bay leaves
1 teaspoon salt
⅛ teaspoon pepper

Sauté onion in butter in a medium saucepan over low heat until tender; add flour, stirring until smooth. Cook 1 minute, stirring constantly. Gradually add beef broth; cook over medium heat, stirring constantly, until thickened and bubbly. Add remaining ingredients; cook over medium heat 5 minutes, stirring occasionally. Remove cloves and bay leaves before serving. Yield: about 4 cups.

*Dinner's on! Sweet-and-Sour Brisket with Sauerkraut.*

## SWEET-AND-SOUR BRISKET WITH SAUERKRAUT

½ teaspoon garlic salt
¼ teaspoon pepper
1 (3- to 4-pound) beef brisket
1 cup water
1 (12-ounce) bottle chili
  sauce
1 (10-ounce) jar apricot
  preserves
2 (16-ounce) cans chopped
  sauerkraut, drained
Celery leaves (optional)

Rub garlic salt and pepper over surface of brisket. Place in a large Dutch oven; add water. Bring to a boil; reduce heat. Cover and simmer 30 minutes.

Combine chili sauce and preserves; pour over brisket. Cover and simmer 1 hour and 15 minutes. Add sauerkraut; cover and cook 15 minutes.

Transfer brisket to a warm serving platter; cut diagonally across the grain into thin slices. Spoon sauerkraut mixture around brisket. Garnish with celery leaves, if desired. Yield: about 10 servings.

The Secret Diary of William Byrd of Westover, 1709 - 1712 is a fascinating reference work for the student of food — and psychology. This eccentric, intellectual aristocrat was a food faddist who usually had only milk for breakfast and preferred to eat only one food at a meal, although it is certain that Westover's table was as well provendered as any in Virginia. For dinner, Byrd could choose from beef roasted, boiled, broiled, hashed, or dried — and sometimes steak, roast veal, tongue, or calf's head.

Byrd breakfasted on milk, except for rare indulgences in rice-milk, broth, custard, hominy, boiled rice, and ingenious combinations like toast and canary (wine) or oysters and chocolate.

## CHUCK WAGON POT ROAST

1 (2- to 3-pound) boneless
   chuck roast
¼ teaspoon pepper
¼ cup all-purpose flour
¼ cup bacon drippings
1 large onion, sliced and
   separated into rings
1½ cups beef broth
½ cup coffee
3 carrots, scraped and cut
   into 2-inch pieces
2 large potatoes, peeled and
   quartered
1½ teaspoons salt, divided
2 cups water
¼ cup all-purpose flour

Sprinkle roast with pepper;
dredge in ¼ cup flour. Brown
roast on all sides in hot bacon
drippings in a large Dutch oven.

Place onion rings over roast;
add beef broth and coffee. Cover
and simmer 1½ hours or until
meat is tender.

Add carrots, potatoes, and 1
teaspoon salt. Cover and simmer an additional 30 minutes or
until vegetables are tender. Remove roast and vegetables to a
serving dish, reserving cooking
liquid in Dutch oven.

Combine 2 cups water, ¼ cup
flour, and remaining ½ teaspoon salt; blend until smooth.
Stir flour mixture into reserved
cooking liquid. Cook, stirring
constantly using a wire whisk,
until smooth and thickened.
Serve gravy with roast and vegetables. Yield: 6 to 8 servings.

Library of Congress

## ARKANSAS POT ROAST

1 (3- to 4-pound) boneless
  chuck roast
2 cloves garlic, sliced
½ teaspoon salt
¼ teaspoon pepper
2 tablespoons vegetable oil
⅓ cup water
1 tablespoon all-purpose flour
¼ cup water

Make several slits in roast, and stuff with garlic slices. Sprinkle with salt and pepper. Brown roast on all sides in hot oil in a large ovenproof Dutch oven. Pour ⅓ cup water over roast. Cover and bake at 325° for 2 hours or until tender.

Remove roast to a serving platter; keep warm. Combine flour and ¼ cup water; stir until smooth. Pour flour mixture into pan drippings; cook, stirring constantly, until thickened and bubbly. Serve gravy with roast. Yield: 6 to 8 servings.

Left: *Chuck Wagon Pot Roast. Divide meat into natural sections; slice across grain for tenderness.*
Below: *Harry Stewart mans a chuck wagon at the Matador Ranch, Ballard Springs, Texas, 1908.*

I n colonial kitchens, where spit-roasting of meat was carried on practically every day, the miracle was that the meat was not covered with soot. The reason was that stern measures of cleaning were carried out: Coals were removed from the fireplace, and every part of it, including the chimney as high as could be reached, was scrubbed with sand and bran. Spits were scoured, too, and iron pots scoured and scalded.

## OVEN-BARBECUED ROAST

1 (4- to 5-pound) boneless
  chuck roast
¾ cup vegetable oil, divided
1 teaspoon salt
¼ teaspoon pepper
¾ cup all-purpose flour
1 cup water
1 cup vinegar
2 tablespoons Worcestershire
  sauce
2 tablespoons prepared
  mustard
2 tablespoons catsup
8 drops hot sauce

Brush roast on all sides with ¼ cup oil. Sprinkle with salt and pepper. Dredge in flour.

Place roast on rack in a roasting pan. Bake, uncovered, at 375° for 30 minutes. Turn roast over, and continue baking, uncovered, 20 minutes.

Add water to pan; cover and continue baking 45 minutes.

Combine remaining ½ cup oil, vinegar, Worcestershire sauce, mustard, catsup, and hot sauce; stir well. Pour sauce over roast; cover and bake an additional 45 minutes or until meat is tender, basting occasionally with sauce. Transfer roast to a warm serving platter; cut into ¼-inch-thick slices. Yield: 10 to 12 servings.

## SUNDAY DINNER POT ROAST

½ cup diced beef suet
1 cup chopped onion
1 clove garlic, minced
¼ cup all-purpose flour
½ teaspoon salt
¼ teaspoon pepper
1 (5-pound) boneless
  chuck roast
2 (14½-ounce) cans
  whole tomatoes,
  undrained
1 tablespoon vinegar
1 tablespoon prepared
  mustard
3 cups water, divided
2 cups uncooked
  macaroni
2 tablespoons all-purpose
  flour

Heat diced beef suet in a large Dutch oven over low heat until crisp. Remove beef suet and discard; reserve beef suet drippings in Dutch oven. Add chopped onion and minced garlic; sauté until tender. Remove onion and garlic with a slotted spoon, and set aside. Reserve drippings in Dutch oven.

Combine ¼ cup flour, salt, and pepper; dredge roast in flour mixture. Brown roast on all sides in reserved drippings. Set Dutch oven aside.

Combine tomatoes, vinegar, mustard, and 2 cups water; mix well. Pour tomato mixture over roast in Dutch oven. Cover and simmer 2½ hours or until meat is tender.

Cook macaroni according to package directions; drain and set aside.

Remove roast to a serving platter, and keep warm; reserve tomato mixture in Dutch oven.

Combine 2 tablespoons flour and remaining 1 cup water, stirring until smooth. Add flour mixture to tomato mixture; cook, stirring constantly, until mixture is thickened and bubbly. Add reserved onion, garlic, and cooked macaroni to tomato gravy; heat thoroughly.

Cut roast into serving pieces; serve with hot macaroni sauce. Yield: 8 to 10 servings.

# CREOLE POT ROAST

¼ cup all-purpose flour
¼ teaspoon salt
¼ teaspoon pepper
1 (3- to 4-pound) chuck roast
2 tablespoons vegetable oil
1 (3-ounce) jar
   pimiento-stuffed
   olives, undrained
2 medium onions, sliced
1½ cups tomato puree
½ cup water
Hot cooked rice
Hot sauce

Combine flour, salt, and pepper; dredge chuck roast in flour mixture. Brown the roast on all sides in hot oil in a large Dutch oven.

Slice olives, reserving liquid. Place sliced olives and onion on top of roast. Combine tomato puree, water, and reserved olive liquid; pour over roast. Cover and simmer 2½ hours or until meat is tender.

Remove roast to a warm serving platter; spoon pan drippings over roast. Serve with hot cooked rice and hot sauce. Yield: 8 to 10 servings.

# BEEF À LA MODE

1 (4-pound) top round roast
4 slices bacon, halved
2 tablespoons all-purpose
   flour
1 teaspoon salt
1 teaspoon pepper
2 tablespoons bacon
   drippings
2 cups water
2 carrots, scraped and
   chopped
2 stalks celery, chopped
1 medium onion, chopped
1 turnip, peeled and diced

Insert blade of sharp knife horizontally through side of roast cutting a 1½-inch wide slit through roast; remove blade. Repeat procedure 8 times, spacing slits evenly in roast. Lay half a slice of bacon on a narrow metal spatula allowing about 1 inch of bacon to extend over end of spatula. Slide spatula completely through slit in roast. Hold bacon slice securely and remove spatula, leaving bacon slice in roast. Repeat procedure with remaining slices of bacon. (A larding needle may be used to insert bacon into roast.)

Combine flour, salt, and pepper; rub over surface of roast. Brown roast on all sides in bacon drippings in a large Dutch oven. Add water. Cover and simmer 1½ hours. Add vegetables; cover and simmer 1 additional hour. Transfer meat and vegetables to a serving platter. Pour pan drippings over meat and vegetables. Yield: 8 to 10 servings.

*Creole Pot Roast appeals to the senses, all the way from its aroma to the tasty melding of its colorful sauce with hot cooked rice.*

## PLEASANT HILL ROUND OF BEEF

1 (3- to 4-pound) boneless
  bottom round roast
3 tablespoons Worcestershire
  sauce
1 tablespoon salt
5 cups water
Horseradish Sauce

Place roast on a roasting rack in a large Dutch oven. Sprinkle Worcestershire sauce and salt over roast. Pour water around roast. Cover and bake at 350° for 1 hour. Uncover and bake an additional 1 hour or until meat is tender, basting often. Transfer roast to a platter, and serve with Horseradish Sauce. Yield: 8 to 10 servings.

Horseradish Sauce:

½ cup whipping cream,
  whipped
½ cup mayonnaise
10 drops hot sauce
⅓ cup prepared horseradish,
  drained
¼ teaspoon Worcestershire
  sauce
⅛ teaspoon dry mustard

Gently combine whipped cream and mayonnaise. Fold in hot sauce, horseradish, Worcestershire sauce, and mustard. Yield: about 1 cup.

## GERMAN POT ROAST AND VEGETABLES

3 tablespoons shortening
1 (3- to 4-pound) boneless
  rump roast
1½ teaspoons salt
½ teaspoon pepper
1 medium onion, peeled and
  sliced
1 small green pepper, diced
6 medium carrots, scraped
  and cut into 1-inch slices
3 medium potatoes, peeled
  and quartered
¼ cup all-purpose flour
1 cup water

Melt shortening in a large Dutch oven over medium heat. Add roast, and brown roast on all sides; sprinkle with salt and pepper. Top meat with onion, green pepper, carrots, and potatoes. Cover and bake at 300° for 2 hours or until meat is tender.

Remove roast and vegetables to a serving platter; reserve pan drippings in Dutch oven. Combine flour and water; stir until smooth. Pour flour mixture into pan drippings. Cook over low heat, stirring constantly, until thickened and bubbly. Serve gravy with roast and vegetables. Yield: 8 to 10 servings.

## DAUBE ROAST

1 clove garlic, minced
1 bay leaf, crushed
1 tablespoon dried parsley
  flakes
2 teaspoons salt
½ teaspoon pepper
⅛ teaspoon red pepper
1 (4-pound) boneless rump
  roast
2 medium onions, chopped
1 tablespoon shortening,
  melted
2 cups water
3 large carrots, scraped and
  sliced
3 green onions, sliced
1 shallot, chopped
1 turnip, peeled and diced
1 cup green peas

Combine first 6 ingredients. Make several small slits in roast. Rub spice mixture into slits and on outside of roast.

Sauté onion in shortening in a large Dutch oven until tender. Add roast, and brown on all sides. Add water; cover and simmer 1 hour.

Stir in carrots, green onion, shallot, turnip, and peas. Cover and simmer 1 hour or until meat and vegetables are tender. Transfer roast to a warm serving platter, and serve with vegetables. Yield: 10 servings.

*Early 1900s ad for ranges.*

## STOVE-TOP POT ROAST

1 (4- to 5-pound) boneless
  sirloin tip roast
3 stalks celery, cut into
  2-inch pieces
1 teaspoon salt
¼ teaspoon pepper
½ teaspoon dry mustard
¼ cup water
6 medium-size red potatoes,
  peeled and cubed
¼ cup vegetable oil
4 medium onions, quartered
2 (14½-ounce) cans stewed
  tomatoes, drained

Combine roast, celery, salt, pepper, mustard, and water in a large Dutch oven. Bring to a boil; cover and simmer 2 hours.

Sauté potatoes in oil in a heavy skillet over medium heat until browned. Add potatoes to roast, reserving pan drippings in skillet. Sauté onion in reserved pan drippings until lightly browned. Add onion and tomatoes to roast. Cover and cook over medium heat 30 minutes or until vegetables are tender. Transfer roast to a platter, and serve with vegetables. Yield: 8 to 10 servings.

# SPICED, PICKLED, AND DRIED

## CORNED BEEF

1 (3- to 4-pound) brisket
1 cup salt
2 tablespoons whole mixed
   pickling spice
½ teaspoon sugar
Pinch of alum
1 clove garlic, minced

Place brisket in a large plastic, glass, or stainless steel container with a tight-fitting lid; cover with water. Add remaining ingredients, stirring until salt dissolves. Cover and marinate 21 days in the refrigerator, turning meat occasionally.

Remove brisket from marinade; discard marinade.

Place brisket in a large Dutch oven with water to cover. Bring to a boil. Reduce heat; cover and simmer 2½ hours. Remove from heat; let stand, without removing cover, for 2 hours.

Remove brisket from cooking liquid; discard cooking liquid. Rinse brisket in cool water; drain. Firmly press entire surface of brisket to remove remaining cooking liquid. Cover and refrigerate.

Cut corned beef diagonally across the grain into thin slices for sandwiches or follow specific recipe directions for preparing corned beef. Yield: 10 servings.

*Corned beef — "and cabbage" or in a lusty Reuben sandwich.*

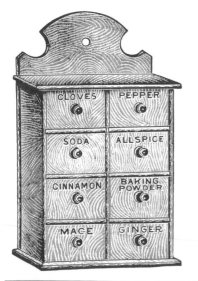

Long before refrigeration, ways were devised for storing and keeping meat. Pickling in brine was one way; packing in a dry mixture of salt, saltpeter, and spices was another. Then there was drying; the oldest cookbooks faithfully gave the directions because that chapter was probably the most important in the book. Corning was a choice method for brisket as well as for tongue. Collaring is an old-time procedure wherein the brisket is rubbed with salt and saltpeter, rolled up, and aged up to a fortnight; then it is washed, re-rolled with herbs and spices, and boiled for hours. The German sauerbraten (sour beef) uses vinegar or wine instead of salt and is meant for short-term keeping.

# MARYLAND CORNED BEEF DINNER

1 (3- to 4-pound) corned beef brisket, trimmed
1 chile pepper
1 bay leaf
1 teaspoon ground mace
1 teaspoon ground cloves
1 teaspoon ground cinnamon
8 new potatoes, unpeeled
6 whole boiling onions
4 stalks celery, cut into 1-inch pieces
4 medium carrots, scraped and cut into 1-inch pieces
1 medium cabbage, cut into wedges

Place brisket in a large Dutch oven with water to cover; add spices. Bring to a boil. Reduce heat; cover and simmer 2½ hours or until brisket is tender.

Add potatoes, onions, celery, and carrots; cover and simmer 20 minutes. Add cabbage; cover and simmer an additional 20 minutes or until vegetables are tender.

Remove brisket to a warm serving platter; cut diagonally across the grain into thin slices. Remove vegetables from cooking liquid; discard cooking liquid and bay leaf. Place vegetables on platter with sliced brisket. Yield: 6 to 8 servings.

# QUICK SAUERBRATEN

1 (4-pound) chuck roast
2 tablespoons vegetable oil
3 tablespoons brown sugar
1 teaspoon ground ginger
⅛ teaspoon ground cloves
⅛ teaspoon ground allspice
1 bay leaf
1½ teaspoons salt
1 teaspoon coarsely ground pepper
¾ cup chopped onion
1½ cups water, divided
⅔ cup red wine vinegar
2 to 4 tablespoons all-purpose flour

Brown roast on both sides in hot oil in a large Dutch oven. Combine sugar, ginger, cloves, allspice, bay leaf, salt, pepper, onion, 1 cup water, and vinegar; mix well, and pour over roast. Cover and simmer 1½ to 2 hours or until roast is tender, turning once. Remove roast to serving platter.

Stir remaining water into flour; stir into pan drippings. Cook, stirring constantly, until thickened. Pour over roast. Yield: 5 to 6 servings.

*Decorative hand-carved butter mold.*

# SALZBURGER SAUERBRATEN

1 (4-pound) chuck roast
3 cups dry red wine
1 large onion, sliced
1 cup diced celery
¾ cup diced carrots
12 whole peppercorns
6 bay leaves
4 whole cloves
2 teaspoons salt
¼ cup plus 2 tablespoons shortening, divided
¼ cup all-purpose flour
1 tablespoon sugar
10 gingersnaps, finely crushed

Place roast in a very large plastic, glass, or stainless steel container. Combine wine, onion, celery, carrots, peppercorns, bay leaves, cloves, and salt; mix well, and pour over roast. Cover and refrigerate 5 days, turning roast each day.

Remove roast from marinade; pat dry. Strain marinade, reserving marinade liquid; set aside. Discard vegetables and spices.

Melt 2 tablespoons shortening in a large Dutch oven; brown roast on all sides. Add reserved marinade liquid. Bring to a boil. Reduce heat; cover and simmer over low heat 2 hours or until roast is tender. Remove roast to a warm serving platter, reserving pan liquid in Dutch oven.

Melt remaining ¼ cup shortening in a large skillet; add flour and sugar. Cook, stirring constantly, until flour is browned. Gradually add 1½ cups reserved pan liquid, stirring with a wire whisk. Cook over medium heat, stirring constantly, until gravy is thickened and bubbly.

Combine gravy with remaining pan liquid in Dutch oven, mixing well. Add gingersnap crumbs; cook, stirring constantly, until smooth and thickened. Spoon gravy over roast. Yield: 8 servings.

Photographer: Jim Bathie

Few men in Southern history have been closer to the seats of power than John Overton. Virginia-born, he moved to Kentucky in 1786 to study law and, in 1789, moved to Nashville where he shared a room and a law practice with Andrew Jackson who was to become his closest friend.

Overton began building his home in 1798 on the site of a fourteenth-century Indian village. He called it Golgotha but later renamed it Travellers' Rest. As Judge of Tennessee's State Superior Court, 1804-1810, Overton wrote opinions that set judicial precedent. He died in 1833 at Travellers' Rest, where he had entertained practically every contemporary person of consequence in the United States. The home and its outbuildings, such as the smokehouse (right), were restored in 1966.

## TENNESSEE SPICED
## ROUND OF BEEF

1 (12-pound) spiced beef
 round
1 cup sorghum molasses
Chopped fresh parsley
 (optional)
Ripe olives (optional)
Pimiento-stuffed olives
 (optional)
Spiced crabapples (optional)
Horseradish-Mustard Sauce
 (page 128)

Soak beef round in cold water
1 hour; drain and rinse well.
Wrap beef securely in cheesecloth; place on a rack in a large
stock pot, and cover with water.
Add molasses; bring to a boil.
Reduce heat; cover and simmer
3 hours or until beef is tender.
(Allow 15 minutes of cooking
time per pound of meat.)

Remove stock pot from heat;
set aside. Allow beef to cool completely in cooking liquid in stock
pot. Remove from cooking liquid; discard cooking liquid.
Chill beef round overnight. Remove cheesecloth. Trim dar-
kened outside areas.

Transfer beef round to a serving platter. Cover top with parsley, and garnish with olives and
crabapples, if desired. Cut diagonally across the grain into
thin slices; serve with Horseradish-Mustard Sauce. Yield: 24 to
36 servings.

*Note:* Commercial spiced beef
round is a specialty in the middle Tennessee area. Usually
served during the Christmas
season, the larded and spiced
beef round may also be pur-
chased ready to serve. A platter
of spiced round often appears
on holiday tables such as the
one at Travellers' Rest pictured
on page 6.

## VIRGINIA SPICED
## BEEF ROUND

1 (11- to 12-pound) beef
 round
2 tablespoons plus 1
 teaspoon saltpeter
2 cups plus 2 tablespoons
 salt, divided
2 cups molasses
2 tablespoons ground allspice
2 tablespoons ground cloves
1½ tablespoons ground
 nutmeg
Spiced crabapples (optional)

Rub meat on all sides with
saltpeter and 2 tablespoons salt;
place in a large plastic, glass, or
stainless steel container with a
tight-fitting lid.

Combine remaining 2 cups
salt, molasses, allspice, cloves,
and nutmeg, stirring well. Pour
molasses mixture over meat;
turn meat to evenly coat all
sides. Cover and marinate 21
days in the refrigerator, turning
meat each day.

Remove meat from marinade;
discard marinade. Wrap securely in cheesecloth, and place
in a large stock pot; cover completely with water. Bring to a
boil. Reduce heat; cover and
simmer 3 hours or until meat is
tender.

Remove stock pot from heat;
set aside. Allow meat to cool
completely in cooking liquid in
stock pot. Remove meat from
cooking liquid, discarding cooking liquid. Chill overnight. Remove cheesecloth.

Transfer meat to a serving
platter. Cut diagonally across
the grain into thin slices to
serve. Yield: 24 to 36 servings.

## BEEF JERKY

1 (1- to 2-pound) flank steak
3 tablespoons salt

Cut steak with the grain in
long strips no more than ¼-inch
thick. Place in a plastic, glass,
or stainless steel container with
a tight fitting lid. Sprinkle with
salt; toss to coat evenly. Cover;
refrigerate at least 24 hours.

Remove meat from container;
wash meat thoroughly with hot
water. Drain well.

Prepare charcoal fire in
smoker, and let burn 10 to 15
minutes. Place water pan in
smoker, and fill with water.

Place meat on food rack; place
rack in smoker. Cover smoker
with lid. Smoke about 12 hours,
refilling water pan with additional water, if needed. Yield: ¼
to ½ pound of dried beef.

## CHIPPED BEEF
## ON TOAST

1 (5-ounce) jar dried beef, cut
 into ½-inch slices
¼ cup butter or margarine
¼ cup plus 2 tablespoons
 all-purpose flour
3 cups milk
Toast points

Sauté dried beef in butter in a
large skillet over low heat 8 minutes or until slightly crisp.
Sprinkle flour evenly over meat;
stir well. Gradually add milk,
stirring until well blended.

Cook over low heat 10 minutes or until thickened and bubbly, stirring often. Serve
chipped beef over toast points.
Yield: 4 to 6 servings.

# STEAKS: PRIME AND CHOICE

## TEXAS STEAK

2 (1½-pound) sirloin
  steaks
1 tablespoon butter or
  margarine, melted
1 teaspoon salt
1 teaspoon pepper

Place steaks on grill 5 inches from hot coals. Grill about 10 minutes on each side or until desired degree of doneness. Brush steaks with butter; sprinkle with salt and pepper. Transfer to a warm serving plate. Yield: 2 to 4 servings.

## STEAK À LA PITCHFORK

2 (1½-pound) sirloin steaks, 1
  inch thick
Salt and pepper to taste
Lemon juice

Place steaks on grill 5 inches from hot coals; grill 8 to 12 minutes on each side or until desired degree of doneness. Season with salt and pepper to taste. Transfer steaks to a warm serving platter, and sprinkle with lemon juice. Yield: 2 to 4 servings.

## PLANKED STEAK

½ teaspoon salt
¼ teaspoon pepper
1 (1½-pound) porterhouse
  steak, 1½ inches thick
1 tablespoon vegetable oil
½ cup kosher salt
Hot mashed potatoes

Sprinkle salt and pepper over steak. Brown steak on one side in hot oil in a skillet. Place steak, browned side down, on a baking sheet; surround steak with kosher salt. Place in oven 5 to 6 inches from heat. Broil 12 minutes or until done.

Place steak on a wooden plank; discard kosher salt. Slice steak; surround with mashed potatoes. Yield: 4 servings.

*A Virginia farmer and his "Pride of the Herd" pose for the cameraman. Surely this Jersey bull was halter-broken to have posed so dutifully.*

## PAN-BROILED FILET MIGNON

1 (4-pound) beef tenderloin
12 slices bacon
2 tablespoons olive oil
1 clove garlic, minced
4 drops hot sauce

Cut beef tenderloin into twelve 1½-inch-thick slices. Trim excess fat from slices. Wrap 1 slice bacon around edge of each steak, and secure with a wooden pick.

Combine oil, garlic, and hot sauce; brush on steaks.

Place steaks, 3 to 4 at a time, in a large skillet. Cook over medium heat 10 minutes or until desired degree of doneness, turning frequently. Serve steak plain or with a butter sauce, if desired. Yield: 12 servings.

## HOTEL ROANOKE STEAK DIANE

2 (4-ounce) filets mignons, ½-inch thick
2 tablespoons chopped onion
2 tablespoons chopped mushrooms
1 tablespoon butter or margarine
2 tablespoons brandy
½ teaspoon dry mustard
⅛ teaspoon salt
⅛ teaspoon pepper
½ teaspoon Worcestershire sauce
¼ cup Burgundy or other dry red wine

Pound steaks to ¼-inch thickness; set aside.

Sauté onion and mushrooms in butter in a heavy skillet over medium heat for 1 minute, stirring frequently. Add steaks; cook 1 minute on each side.

Heat brandy in a small pan until just warm. Pour over steaks; ignite with a long match. When flames die down, remove steaks; set aside.

Add mustard, salt, pepper, and Worcestershire sauce to mushroom mixture; blend well. Return steaks to skillet; add wine. Simmer over low heat 5

minutes or until desired degree of doneness. Remove steaks to a warm serving plate; pour wine sauce over steaks. Serve immediately. Yield: 1 to 2 servings.

## BROILED STEAK WITH MUSHROOM-WINE SAUCE

1 (2-pound) boneless top sirloin steak, 2 inches thick
¼ pound fresh mushrooms, sliced
2 tablespoons finely chopped onion
1 clove garlic, minced
2 tablespoons butter or margarine
2 teaspoons all-purpose flour
2 tablespoons tomato paste
½ teaspoon salt
⅛ teaspoon pepper
½ cup dry red wine
¼ cup water

Place sirloin on a well-greased rack in a shallow roasting pan about 5 inches from heating element. Broil 10 minutes on each side or until desired degree of doneness. Remove steak to a warm serving platter.

Sauté mushrooms, onion, and garlic in butter in a medium saucepan over low heat until vegetables are tender. Add flour; stir until smooth. Cook over medium heat 1 minute, stirring constantly.

Add tomato paste, salt, and pepper; stir until well blended. Gradually add wine and water, stirring constantly until well blended. Cover and cook over low heat 20 minutes. Spoon sauce over steak to serve. Yield: 6 servings.

*Late nineteenth-century ad promotes beef extract.*

## SPANISH STEAK

1 (5-pound) sirloin steak
1 teaspoon salt
½ teaspoon pepper
½ cup catsup
½ cup chili sauce
½ teaspoon Worcestershire sauce
1 medium onion, peeled and sliced
1 medium-size green pepper, seeded and sliced into rings
1 lemon, sliced
2 tablespoons butter or margarine
1 cup hot water

Sprinkle steak with salt and pepper. Place in a greased 13- x 9- x 2-inch baking dish. Insert meat thermometer, if desired.

Combine catsup, chili sauce, and Worcestershire sauce; pour over steak. Place onion, green pepper, and lemon slices on top of steak. Dot with butter. Pour water around steak.

Bake at 400° for 1 hour or until meat thermometer registers 140° (rare). Discard lemon slices. Yield: 8 servings.

## CARPETBAG STEAK

2 (1½-pound) strip steaks, cut
  with pockets
1 (12-ounce) container fresh
  Select or Standard oysters,
  drained
½ teaspoon salt
¼ teaspoon pepper
Maître d'Hôtel Butter

Stuff each pocket of steak
with half the oysters; secure
openings with wooden picks.
Sprinkle each steak with salt
and pepper.

Place steaks on rack in a
broiler pan. Place pan 5 to 6
inches from heating element.
Broil steaks 8 to 10 minutes on
each side or until desired degree
of doneness. To serve, slice diagonally across the grain. Serve
steaks with Maître d'Hôtel Butter. Yield: 4 to 6 servings.

### Maître d'Hôtel Butter:

½ cup butter
2 tablespoons lemon
  juice
2 tablespoons chopped
  fresh parsley
¼ teaspoon salt
Dash of pepper
Dash of hot sauce

Melt butter over low heat in a
small saucepan; stir in remaining ingredients. Serve warm.
Yield: about ¾ cup.

*Carpetbag Steak, packed
with oysters, traveling with
Maître d'Hôtel Butter. A
combination to do justice
to a grand occasion.*

## OKLAHOMA
## FLANK STEAK

1 (1¼-pound) flank steak
1 tablespoon vegetable oil
2 tablespoons finely chopped
  green pepper
2 tablespoons finely chopped
  carrot
2 tablespoons finely chopped
  celery
2 teaspoons salt
½ teaspoon pepper
1 bay leaf
1 clove garlic, minced
2 cups hot water
4 medium potatoes, peeled
  and quartered
1 tablespoon all-purpose flour

Pound steak to ¼-inch thickness; rub steak with oil. Brown
on both sides over medium-high
heat in an ovenproof Dutch
oven. Add next 8 ingredients.
Cover; bake at 350° for 1½
hours. Add potatoes; bake an
additional 30 minutes.

Remove steak and potatoes to
a serving platter; reserve pan
drippings in Dutch oven. Remove bay leaf.

Combine flour and a small
amount of water; stir until
smooth. Pour mixture into pan
drippings. Cook over low heat,
stirring constantly, until thickened. Spoon over steak and vegetables. To serve, cut steak
diagonally across grain into
thin slices. Yield: 4 servings.

## FRUITED
## STEAK ROLL

1 (1½-pound) flank steak
1 large tart apple, peeled,
  cored, and chopped
1 cup soft breadcrumbs
¼ cup chopped onion
2 tablespoons chopped celery
1 teaspoon salt
½ teaspoon rubbed sage
1 tablespoon bacon drippings
1 cup hot water
1 tablespoon apple cider
  vinegar
1 (8-ounce) package prunes

Pound steak to ⅛-inch thickness. Combine apple, breadcrumbs, onion, celery, salt, and
sage. Spoon stuffing onto steak,
spreading to within ½ inch of
edge. Roll up jellyroll fashion; tie
with string to secure stuffing.

Brown steak roll on both sides
in hot bacon drippings in a
Dutch oven. Add hot water and
vinegar. Cover and simmer 45
minutes over low heat. Turn
steak roll; add prunes, and simmer an additional 40 minutes or
until steak is tender.

Remove string. Place steak
roll on a serving platter; spoon
prunes around steak. Pour
gravy over steak; slice and serve.
Yield: 4 to 6 servings.

*Digging for potatoes
and other harvesting chores
went better when shared.*

# NEW ORLEANS FLANK STEAK

1 (1-pound) flank steak
¼ cup plus 1 tablespoon
  all-purpose flour, divided
2 tablespoons finely chopped
  onion
3 tablespoons butter or
  margarine
3 tablespoons vinegar
2 cups water
1 teaspoon dry mustard
1 teaspoon dried whole
  thyme
1 teaspoon paprika
1 teaspoon salt
½ teaspoon ground black
  pepper
½ teaspoon red pepper
Chopped fresh parsley
  (optional)

Pound steak to ½-inch thickness. Slice diagonally across the grain into ½-inch-thick slices. Dredge pieces in ¼ cup flour, and set aside.

Sauté onion in butter in a heavy skillet until tender. Add dredged steak pieces to sautéed onion mixture in skillet; brown steak on all sides. Remove steak from pan, reserving sautéed onion and pan drippings.

Add remaining 1 tablespoon flour to reserved pan drippings mixture; cook 1 minute over low heat, stirring constantly. Gradually add vinegar and water; cook over medium heat 1 minute, stirring constantly. Combine mustard, thyme, paprika, salt, and pepper; mix well. Add spices to pan liquid; bring mixture to a boil, stirring until well blended.

Add steak to gravy; cover and simmer 1 hour and 20 minutes or until meat is tender. Transfer to a serving platter. Garnish with parsley, if desired. Yield: 4 servings.

*French meat market, New Orleans. Engraving c.1883.*

## CHICKEN-FRIED STEAK

4 (¼-pound) cubed steaks
¼ teaspoon pepper
1 egg
2 tablespoons water
1 cup all-purpose flour
Vegetable oil
½ teaspoon salt

Sprinkle steaks with pepper; set aside. Combine egg and water, mixing well. Dredge steak in flour, and dip in egg mixture. Dredge again in flour.

Heat ½ inch of oil to 350°; add steak, and fry 10 minutes or until golden brown, turning once. Drain steak on paper towels. Sprinkle with salt before serving. Yield: 4 servings.

A Texan tends to differentiate between country-fried steak and chicken-fried steak. Country-fried is fondly remembered as what Mother used to make by pounding flour and seasonings into round steak and then frying it in an iron skillet. Cream gravy was made from the fat and crumbs left in the pan. Chicken-fried steak is what a Texan ate in restaurants. The meat was coated with seasoned flour, dipped in egg, and then again in flour. Deep fried it was: no gravy.

*Longhorns near Iredell, Texas, in* Old Chisholm Trail *by Clara McDonald Williamson, 1952.*

## ON THE TRAIL COUNTRY-FRIED STEAK

2 pounds boneless round steak
⅓ cup all-purpose flour
¼ teaspoon pepper
¼ cup vegetable oil
Salt to taste
2 tablespoons all-purpose flour
½ cup evaporated milk
¼ cup coffee
¼ cup water
¼ teaspoon salt
⅛ teaspoon pepper

Trim excess fat from steak. Pound steak to ¼-inch thickness; cut into 6 serving-size pieces.

Combine ⅓ cup flour and ¼ teaspoon pepper. Dredge steak in flour mixture. Lightly pound floured steak. Heat oil in a large skillet over medium heat. Add steak; cover and cook 10 minutes. Uncover and cook an additional 5 minutes, turning to brown evenly. Remove steak, reserving pan drippings in skillet. Drain steak. Sprinkle with salt to taste.

Add 2 tablespoons flour to drippings, stirring until smooth. Cook over low heat 1 minute, stirring constantly. Gradually add milk, coffee, and water; cook over medium heat, stirring constantly, until thickened and bubbly. Stir in ¼ teaspoon salt and ⅛ teaspoon pepper. Serve gravy with steak. Yield: 6 servings.

## CUBED STEAK WITH ONION

4 (¼-pound) cubed steaks
¼ cup milk
1 cup self-rising flour
¾ teaspoon salt
¼ teaspoon pepper
¼ cup shortening
4 (¼-inch-thick) slices onion

Brush steaks with milk. Combine flour, salt, and pepper. Dredge steaks in flour mixture, coating well.

Heat shortening in a heavy skillet over medium heat. Brown steaks on one side until golden brown. Turn steaks, and place a slice of onion on each piece. Reduce heat; cover and simmer 25 minutes. Cook, uncovered, an additional 5 minutes. Yield: 4 servings.

*Swiss Steak was a favorite in this Atlanta, Georgia, tearoom, 1930 to 1962.*

## STEAK FINGERS

2 pounds boneless
  round steak
2 eggs
2 tablespoons water
1 cup all-purpose flour
1½ teaspoons salt
1½ teaspoons pepper
½ cup shortening

Trim excess fat from steak; pound steak to ⅛-inch thickness; cut into 4- x 1-inch strips.

Combine eggs and water, beating well. Stir together flour, salt, and pepper. Dip steak strips in egg, and dredge in flour mixture.

Melt shortening in a large skillet. Brown steak fingers on both sides. Reduce heat; cover and simmer 15 minutes or until tender. Serve immediately. Yield: 8 servings.

## GEORGIA TEAROOM SWISS STEAK

1 large onion, chopped
¼ cup vegetable oil, divided
¼ cup all-purpose flour
1½ teaspoons salt
1 teaspoon dry mustard
¼ teaspoon pepper
6 (¼-pound) cubed steaks
1 clove garlic, minced
1 (14½-ounce) can whole
  tomatoes, undrained and
  chopped
Hot mashed potatoes

Sauté onion in 2 tablespoons oil in a large ovenproof skillet until tender; remove sautéed onion, and set aside, reserving drippings in skillet.

Combine flour, salt, mustard, and pepper; dredge steaks in flour mixture.

Brown steaks in reserved drippings plus remaining 2 tablespoons oil; add sautéed onion, garlic, and tomatoes, stirring gently. Cover and bake at 325° for 45 minutes or until meat is tender. Serve immediately over hot mashed potatoes. Yield: 6 servings.

*Jersey milk cows being judged in a local competition, late 1930s.*

# KENTUCKY ROUND STEAK

¼ cup all-purpose flour
½ teaspoon salt
½ teaspoon paprika
¼ teaspoon pepper
1½ pounds boneless round
   steak
2 tablespoons vegetable oil
1 tablespoon lemon juice
1 medium onion, thinly sliced
1 medium-size green pepper,
   seeded and thinly sliced
4 (¼-inch-thick) slices lemon
½ cup water
¼ cup catsup

"Steak that is not porter-house can be improved by treating as the French chefs prepare their steaks to make them tender," according to a writer on Creole cookery in *De Bonnes Choses à Manger.* Thomas Jefferson had, of course, learned the Frenchman's secret for tenderizing meats by marinating them in a combination of olive oil and vinegar, a technique he often used.

Trim excess fat from steak; cut into 6 serving-size pieces.

Combine flour, salt, paprika, and pepper; dredge steak in flour mixture.

Heat oil in a large skillet, and brown steak. Place half of browned steak in the bottom of a lightly greased 1½-quart casserole. Drizzle top of steak with half of lemon juice; top with half of onion and green pepper slices. Repeat layers, and top with lemon slices.

Combine water and catsup, stirring well. Pour over lemon slices. Cover and bake at 325° for 1 hour and 15 minutes or until steak is tender. Discard lemon slices, and serve immediately. Yield: 6 servings.

*Street vendors painted by Nicolina Calyo included this dressy mid-1800s butcher.*

## STEAK BIRDS

1 cup chopped pecans
1 tablespoon finely chopped onion
⅓ cup butter or margarine, melted
2 cups soft breadcrumbs
⅓ cup water
1 teaspoon salt, divided
¼ teaspoon pepper, divided
1 (1-pound) breakfast steak, cut into 8 very thin slices
2 tablespoons vegetable oil
2 tablespoons all-purpose flour
1 cup beef broth

Sauté pecans and onion in butter in a small skillet over low heat until onion is tender. Combine sautéed pecans and onion with breadcrumbs, water, ½ teaspoon salt, and ⅛ teaspoon pepper; mix well.

Place 2 tablespoons stuffing on each piece of steak. Roll up each piece jellyroll fashion and secure with wooden picks. Place steak rolls on a well-greased rack in a shallow roasting pan. Bake at 350° for 25 minutes. Set aside.

Heat oil in a medium saucepan over low heat; add flour, stirring until smooth. Cook 1 minute, stirring constantly. Gradually add beef broth; cook over medium heat, stirring constantly, until thickened and bubbly.

Add remaining ½ teaspoon salt and ⅛ teaspoon pepper; stir well. Pour gravy over steak rolls to serve. Yield: 4 servings.

## BLUE RIBBON ROUND STEAK

4 pounds (¾-inch-thick) boneless round steak
2 tablespoons shortening
½ cup minced onion
¾ cup catsup
¼ cup plus 2 tablespoons water
¼ cup vinegar
1 tablespoon firmly packed brown sugar
1 tablespoon Worcestershire sauce
1 tablespoon prepared mustard
½ teaspoon salt
⅛ teaspoon pepper
Fresh parsley sprigs (optional)
Spiced red apple rings (optional)
Lemon slices (optional)
Red maraschino cherries, cut in half (optional)

Trim excess fat from steak; cut steak into 10 serving-size pieces. Melt shortening in large skillet, and brown steak on each side. Remove meat to a 2½-quart shallow baking dish; set aside. Reserve pan drippings in skillet.

Sauté onion in reserved drippings until tender. Set aside.

Combine catsup, water, vinegar, sugar, Worcestershire sauce, mustard, salt, and pepper. Add catsup mixture to sautéed onion in skillet. Mix well. Simmer 5 minutes, stirring often.

Pour sauce over steak in baking dish. Cover and bake at 350° for 1 hour or until steak is tender. Remove meat to a serving platter. For a "blue ribbon" dish, garnish with parsley and spiced apple rings topped with a lemon slice and a maraschino cherry half, if desired. Yield: 10 servings.

# BEEF ROULADEN

2½ pounds (½-inch-thick)
  round steak
¾ pound ground beef
¼ cup finely crushed cracker
  crumbs
2 tablespoons minced onion
1 teaspoon poultry seasoning
½ clove garlic, crushed
¾ teaspoon salt
3 tablespoons vegetable oil
1½ pounds small boiling
  onions
1 tablespoon bottled brown
  bouquet sauce
⅓ cup all-purpose flour
1 (10½-ounce) can beef broth,
  undiluted
2½ cups Burgundy or other
  dry red wine
1 tablespoon chopped fresh
  parsley (optional)
1 pound fresh mushrooms,
  halved
1 bay leaf
Hot buttered noodles
  (optional)

Trim fat from steak; pound steak to ⅛-inch thickness, and cut into 10 pieces. Set aside.

Combine ground beef, cracker crumbs, onion, poultry seasoning, garlic, and salt; mix well. Place 1 heaping tablespoon stuffing on each piece of steak. Roll up each piece jellyroll fashion; tie each end with string.

Brown beef rolls on all sides in hot oil in large skillet; transfer to a small roasting pan, reserving pan drippings in skillet. Set rouladen aside.

Brown onions in reserved pan drippings. Remove onions to roasting pan; reserve pan drippings in skillet. Set aside.

Combine brown bouquet sauce and pan drippings; add flour, stirring until smooth. Gradually add wine; cook over medium heat, stirring constantly, until thickened.

Pour wine mixture over rouladen and onions; add bay leaf. Top with mushrooms. Cover and bake at 350° for 1 hour. Remove bay leaf before serving. Sprinkle with parsley, and serve with hot buttered noodles, if desired. Yield: 10 servings.

# GREEK-STUFFED BEEF ROLLS

2 to 3 pounds (¼-inch-thick)
  top round steak
1 cup chopped onion
¾ cup chopped carrot
⅔ cup chopped celery
1 clove garlic, minced
½ teaspoon ground cinnamon
½ teaspoon salt
½ teaspoon pepper
2 tablespoons olive oil
4 cups water
1 (6-ounce) can tomato paste
1 teaspoon sugar
½ teaspoon salt
¼ teaspoon pepper
Hot cooked spaghetti

Trim excess fat from steak; cut steak into 4 serving-size pieces. Set aside.

Combine onion, carrot, celery, garlic, cinnamon, ½ teaspoon salt, and ½ teaspoon pepper. Place one-fourth of mixture on each piece of steak. Roll up jellyroll fashion; tie each steak roll with string to secure stuffing.

Brown steak rolls on all sides in hot oil in a large Dutch oven. Drain off oil. Add water; bring to a boil. Reduce heat, and simmer, uncovered, 1 hour. Add tomato paste, sugar, remaining salt, and pepper. Cover and simmer 30 minutes or until tender. Serve steak rolls and sauce over hot cooked spaghetti. Yield: 4 to 6 servings.

*Beef Rouladen: Rolled beef with a German accent.*

## GERMAN STEAK ROLLS

2½ pounds boneless round steak
¾ cup all-purpose flour
½ teaspoon salt
¼ teaspoon pepper
6 (5-inch) strips dill pickle
3 slices bacon, cut in half, sliced crosswise
Vegetable oil
½ cup water
¼ cup Worcestershire sauce

Trim excess fat from steak; cut into 6 serving-size pieces, and set aside.

Combine flour, salt, and pepper; mix well. Dredge steaks in seasoned flour. Place 1 dill pickle strip and 1 bacon half on each piece of steak. Roll up each piece jellyroll fashion; secure with a wooden pick.

Brown steaks in hot oil in a large skillet; transfer steak rolls to a 9-inch square baking dish. Add water and Worcestershire sauce. Cover and bake at 350° for 1 hour and 10 minutes. Spoon sauce over each steak roll before serving. Yield: 6 servings.

*Beef Stroganoff can make a cook's reputation.*

## BEEF STROGANOFF

1½ pounds boneless sirloin steak
¼ cup all-purpose flour
1 teaspoon salt
3 tablespoons vegetable oil
½ pound fresh mushrooms, sliced
1 (10½-ounce) can beef broth
2 tablespoons catsup
2 tablespoons butter or margarine
1 tablespoon Worcestershire sauce
1 teaspoon dry mustard
1 (8-ounce) carton commercial sour cream
Hot buttered noodles

Trim excess fat from steak. Partially freeze steak; slice across grain into 2- x ¼-inch strips.

Combine flour and salt. Dredge steak in flour mixture; sauté in hot oil in a large skillet until browned. Add mushrooms, beef broth, catsup, butter, Worcestershire sauce, and mustard; stir well. Cover and cook over low heat 1 hour. Just before serving, add sour cream; stir until well blended. Serve over hot buttered noodles. Yield: 4 to 6 servings.

## BŒUF BOURGUIGNON

1 medium onion, chopped
¼ cup bacon drippings, divided
⅓ cup all-purpose flour
½ teaspoon salt
¼ teaspoon ground marjoram
¼ teaspoon ground thyme
¼ teaspoon pepper
1 (2-pound) sirloin steak, cut into 1½-inch cubes
¾ cup Burgundy or other dry red wine
¾ cup beef broth
¼ teaspoon hot sauce
½ pound fresh mushrooms, sliced
Hot cooked rice

Sauté onion in 2 tablespoons drippings until tender; drain, reserving drippings. Set aside.

Combine flour, salt, marjoram, thyme, and pepper; mix well. Dredge sirloin cubes in flour mixture; sauté in remaining hot bacon drippings in a large skillet until browned. Add wine, beef broth, and hot sauce, stirring well. Cover and cook over low heat 45 minutes.

Stir in mushrooms; cover and cook 15 minutes. Serve over rice. Yield: 6 servings.

## MEXICAN STEAK

3 pounds boneless round steak
2 large onions, chopped
2 stalks celery, chopped
1 small green pepper, seeded and chopped
1 clove garlic, minced
2 tablespoons chili powder
2 cups (8 ounces) shredded Cheddar cheese

Trim excess fat from steak; cut steak into 4- x 1-inch strips. Place steak strips, onion, celery, green pepper, and garlic in a large Dutch oven. Cook over low heat 30 minutes. Add chili powder; cover and simmer 1 hour or until steak is tender. Stir in cheese; cook 2 minutes or until cheese melts. Serve immediately. Yield: 8 servings.

*Mexican food vendors in open air market, San Antonio's Military Plaza in the 1800s.*

## FAJITAS

2¼ pounds skirt steak,
  ¼-inch thick
1 tablespoon garlic
  salt
Juice of 5 limes
¼ cup vegetable oil
Flour tortillas
Pico de Gallo
Guacamole

Pound steak to ⅛-inch thickness. Sprinkle both sides of steak with garlic salt and lime juice. Cover and refrigerate overnight. Drain well; discard marinade.

Place steak on grill; cook over medium heat 8 to 10 minutes on each side, brushing with oil occasionally. Remove from grill, and cut into thin slices. Serve with flour tortillas, Pico de Gallo, and Guacamole. Yield: 6 to 8 servings.

### Pico de Gallo:

1 (4-ounce) can chopped
  green chiles, drained
2 medium banana peppers,
  finely chopped
5 green onions, chopped
5 medium tomatoes, peeled
  and chopped
¼ cup cilantro
2 tablespoons vegetable
  oil
1 teaspoon vinegar
½ teaspoon salt

Combine all ingredients, mixing well. Cover and refrigerate overnight. Yield: about 4 cups.

*Note:* Sauce may be refrigerated up to 2 weeks.

### Guacamole:

2 medium avocados,
  peeled and mashed
1 small tomato, peeled
  and chopped
2 tablespoons mayonnaise
2 teaspoons finely
  chopped onion
1½ teaspoons lemon
  juice
1 teaspoon garlic powder
¼ teaspoon salt
Dash of pepper

Combine all ingredients, mixing well. Yield: about 2 cups.

# GROUND BEEF SPECIALTIES

## ROLLED MEAT LOAF WITH WALNUTS AND ORANGES

1 egg
⅓ cup milk
2 pounds ground chuck
2 tablespoons finely chopped onion
1½ teaspoons Worcestershire sauce
1½ teaspoons salt
⅛ teaspoon pepper
Stuffing (recipe follows)
½ cup catsup
¼ cup water
Toasted walnut halves
Orange slices

Combine egg and milk in a large mixing bowl, beating well. Add meat, onion, Worcestershire sauce, salt, and pepper; mix well. Shape into a 12- x 10-inch rectangle on a sheet of waxed paper.

Spoon stuffing over beef, leaving a ½-inch margin around edges. Beginning at short end, roll up meat jellyroll fashion, lifting waxed paper to help in rolling. Press seams and ends together to seal.

Place roll, seam side down, in a 13- x 9- x 2-inch baking pan. Combine catsup and water; pour over roll. Bake at 350° for 1 hour and 15 minutes. Remove to a serving platter. Garnish with toasted walnut halves and orange slices. Yield: 8 servings.

**Stuffing:**

3 cups soft breadcrumbs
1½ cups chopped celery
1 cup chopped walnuts
½ cup milk
2 tablespoons finely chopped onion
1 teaspoon salt
¼ teaspoon poultry seasoning
⅛ teaspoon pepper

Combine all ingredients in a large mixing bowl; stir well. Yield: 3 cups.

*Rolled Meat Loaf with Walnuts and Oranges has good things stuffed inside.*

## SHAKERTOWN MEAT LOAF

1½ pounds ground chuck
½ cup finely chopped onion
2 tablespoons diced celery
2 tablespoons diced green
  pepper
1 egg, beaten
1 teaspoon salt
¼ teaspoon pepper
1 cup tomato juice
¾ cup quick-cooking oats,
  uncooked

Combine meat, onion, celery, green pepper, egg, salt, and pepper in a large mixing bowl; mix well. Add tomato juice and oats, mixing well.

Shape meat mixture into a loaf; place on aluminum foil on a broiler rack. Bake at 350° for 1 hour. Yield: 6 servings.

## WELSH MEAT LOAF

1 cup chopped celery
½ cup chopped onion
½ cup chopped green pepper
2 tablespoons chopped fresh
  parsley
2 tablespoons shortening
2 pounds ground chuck
2 cups soft breadcrumbs
2 eggs, beaten
1 cup milk
1 teaspoon salt
½ teaspoon pepper
2 hard-cooked eggs, thinly
  sliced
3 tablespoons fine dry
  breadcrumbs
½ teaspoon paprika

Sauté celery, onion, green pepper, and parsley in shortening in a skillet over low heat until vegetables are tender.

Combine sautéed vegetables, meat, soft breadcrumbs, eggs, milk, salt, and pepper; mix well. Pack half of meat mixture into a 10- x 6- x 2-inch baking dish. Place egg slices on top of mixture. Spoon remaining meat mixture over egg slices; press lightly on sides to seal. Sprinkle dry breadcrumbs and paprika over top. Bake at 350° for 1½ hours. Loaf may be served hot or cold. Yield: 8 servings.

## GERMAN-STYLE MEATBALLS

2 slices bread
½ cup minced onion
1 tablespoon butter or
  margarine
1½ pounds ground chuck
½ pound ground pork
2 eggs, beaten
1 teaspoon salt
⅛ teaspoon nutmeg
3 tablespoons chopped fresh
  parsley
½ teaspoon grated lemon rind
1 teaspoon lemon juice
1 teaspoon Worcestershire
  sauce
5 cups beef broth
½ cup flour
1 cup water
Hot cooked noodles

Tear bread into small pieces, and place in a small shallow bowl. Add water to cover, and let soak about 5 minutes. Squeeze water from bread; discard water. Set bread aside.

Sauté onion in butter until tender. Combine sautéed onion, bread, meat, eggs, salt, nutmeg, parsley, lemon rind, lemon juice, and Worcestershire sauce in a large bowl. Mix well; shape into 2-inch meatballs.

Bring beef broth to a boil in a large Dutch oven; add meatballs. Reduce heat; cover and simmer 15 minutes. Remove meatballs; set aside. Reserve pan liquid.

Combine flour and water, mixing well. Stir flour mixture into reserved pan liquid. Cook over medium-high heat, stirring constantly, until thickened and bubbly.

Return meatballs to Dutch oven; cook over low heat until meatballs are thoroughly heated. Serve meatballs and gravy over hot cooked noodles. Yield: 8 to 10 servings.

*Trade card from late 1800s.*

## BEEF PORCUPINES

1 pound ground chuck
1 cup uncooked regular rice
1½ teaspoons salt, divided
¼ teaspoon pepper, divided
1 small onion, thinly sliced
1 small green pepper, seeded
  and cut into rings
1 small clove garlic, minced
1 tablespoon vegetable oil
1 (24-ounce) can tomato juice

Combine meat and rice in a large bowl. Add 1 teaspoon salt and ⅛ teaspoon pepper, mixing well. Shape mixture into 1½-inch meatballs. Place meatballs in a shallow 2½-quart casserole; set aside.

Sauté onion, green pepper, and garlic in hot oil in a large skillet until tender. Add tomato juice, and remaining salt and pepper; pour sauce over meatballs. Cover and bake at 350° for 1 hour and 15 minutes or until rice is tender, turning meatballs occasionally. Yield: 18 (1½-inch) meatballs.

*Grilled burgers are the all-American food, but this one is the giant of them all. Each serving has cheese hidden inside.*

## GRILLED CHEESEBURGERS

2 pounds ground chuck
1 tablespoon Worcestershire sauce
½ teaspoon garlic powder
⅛ teaspoon hot sauce
½ teaspoon salt
½ teaspoon pepper
1 cup (4 ounces) shredded sharp Cheddar cheese, divided
2 tablespoons butter or margarine, divided
6 slices bacon
⅔ cup commercial barbecue sauce
6 hamburger buns, split
6 lettuce leaves
6 slices onion
6 slices tomato
6 slices pickle
2 tablespoons mayonnaise, divided
2 tablespoons mustard, divided
2 tablespoons catsup, divided

Combine meat, Worcestershire sauce, garlic, hot sauce, salt, and pepper; mix well.

Divide meat into 12 equal portions; shape each portion into a 4-inch pattie. Sprinkle one-sixth of cheese on each of 6 patties. Place 1 teaspoon butter on top of cheese. Top each with 1 of the remaining 6 patties. Press edges of filled patties together to seal. Wrap a slice of bacon around each cheeseburger, and secure with a wooden pick.

Grill over medium coals 12 to 15 minutes or until desired degree of doneness, turning patties and brushing frequently with barbecue sauce.

Place 1 cheeseburger on bottom of each bun. Top each with lettuce leaf, onion, tomato, and pickle slices, and 1 teaspoon each of mayonnaise, mustard, and catsup. Cover with tops of buns. Yield: 6 servings.

## HAMBURGER STEAK DELUXE

2 pounds ground sirloin
1 (10¾-ounce) can chicken broth
1 egg, beaten
2 tablespoons Worcestershire sauce
1 teaspoon salt
½ teaspoon pepper
½ teaspoon Dijon mustard
Dash of hot sauce
2 tablespoons shortening
Sauce (recipe follows)

Combine first 8 ingredients in a large bowl; mix well. Shape mixture into 8 patties.

Melt shortening in a large skillet over medium heat. Cook patties 10 minutes, turning once. Drain. Pour sauce over each to serve. Yield: 8 servings.

Sauce:

1 (12-ounce) jar prepared brown gravy or 1½ cups brown beef gravy
½ cup catsup
1 tablespoon Worcestershire sauce
1 tablespoon Dijon mustard
1 tablespoon butter or margarine
2 tablespoons chopped fresh parsley

Combine first 5 ingredients in a heavy saucepan. Bring to a boil. Reduce heat, and simmer 10 minutes. Remove from heat; stir in parsley. Yield: 2½ cups.

"Grind good round steak in a meat mill, and make into loaves four inches square, and three quarters of an inch thick," begins the recipe for Hamburg Steaks in the *Annie Dennis Cook Book*, 1901. No, she didn't serve them on buns with "everything" on them; they were soaked in melted butter and served hot.

## MOCK FILET MIGNON

2 slices bread
1¼ cups water, divided
1 pound ground chuck
½ teaspoon seasoned salt
½ teaspoon pepper
6 slices bacon
2 tablespoons shortening
2 tablespoons catsup
1 tablespoon Worcestershire sauce

Tear bread into small pieces, and place in a small, shallow bowl. Add ½ cup water, and let soak about 10 minutes. Squeeze water from bread; discard water.

Combine softened bread, meat, seasoned salt, and pepper in a medium bowl; mix well. Shape mixture into 6 patties about ½-inch thick. Wrap a bacon slice around each pattie, securing with a wooden pick. Melt shortening in a large skillet over medium heat. Cook patties until brown on each side.

Place patties in a lightly greased 2½-quart shallow baking dish. Combine ¾ cup water, catsup, and Worcestershire sauce; stir well. Pour sauce over patties; cover and bake at 350° for 1 hour. Yield: 6 servings.

## MOCK CHICKEN-FRIED STEAKS

1½ pounds ground chuck
2 eggs, beaten
⅓ cup cracker crumbs
1 teaspoon salt
½ teaspoon pepper
⅛ teaspoon garlic powder
2 eggs, beaten
1 cup all-purpose flour
⅓ cup vegetable oil
1 tablespoon all-purpose flour
1 cup milk

Combine first 6 ingredients in a large mixing bowl; mix well. Shape mixture into 6 patties.

Dip each patty in beaten egg; dredge in flour. Fry patties in hot oil in a large skillet until golden brown, turning once. Drain on paper towels. Transfer patties to a serving platter, and keep warm.

Drain off pan drippings, reserving 2 tablespoons in skillet. Stir in 1 tablespoon flour; cook over medium heat, scraping sides of skillet with a wooden spoon to loosen browned crumbs. Gradually add milk, stirring constantly, until thickened and bubbly. Serve gravy with steaks. Yield: 6 servings.

## CAJUN SPECIAL

2 pounds ground chuck
½ teaspoon salt
½ teaspoon coarsely ground black pepper
¼ cup olive oil
¼ cup brandy
1 cup whipping cream
1 (7-ounce) package wild pecan rice, cooked

Shape meat into 4 patties; sprinkle salt and pepper over surface of patties. Cook patties in oil in a large skillet 10 minutes or until desired degree of doneness. Transfer patties to a serving platter, and keep warm. Reserve 2 tablespoons pan drippings in skillet.

Place brandy in a small pan; heat just until warm. Pour brandy over pan drippings, and ignite. Flame 1 minute; add whipping cream, and cook over low heat, stirring frequently, 5 minutes or until slightly thickened. Pour sauce over steaks, and serve with wild pecan rice. Yield: 4 servings.

*In Louisville, Kentucky, Little Taverns offered courtesy service and five-cent hamburgers you could "Buy-By-Bag."*

Photographic Archives, University of Louisville

*Worker stirs beans in cooker at Gebhardt Chili Powder Co. in San Antonio.*

## CREOLE BEEF

3 tablespoons finely chopped onion
¼ cup bacon drippings
1½ pounds ground chuck
2 (14½-ounce) cans whole tomatoes, undrained and chopped
¼ cup plus 2 tablespoons chopped green pepper
1 tablespoon Worcestershire sauce
1 teaspoon sugar
1 teaspoon salt
¼ teaspoon pepper
Hot cooked rice

Sauté onion in drippings in a heavy skillet over low heat until tender. Add meat; cook over low heat until meat is browned, stirring to crumble. Drain off pan drippings; discard.

Add tomatoes, green pepper, Worcestershire sauce, sugar, salt, and pepper, mixing well. Cook, uncovered, over low heat 45 minutes, stirring occasionally. Serve over hot cooked rice. Yield: 6 servings.

## TEXAS GROUND BEEF HASH

2 large onions, thinly sliced and separated into rings
2 medium-size green peppers, seeded and chopped
3 tablespoons shortening, melted
1 pound ground chuck
1 (14½-ounce) can whole tomatoes, undrained and chopped
½ cup uncooked regular rice
1 teaspoon chili powder
1 teaspoon salt
¼ teaspoon pepper
¼ teaspoon celery salt

Sauté onion and green pepper in shortening over low heat until tender. Add meat; cook over low heat until meat is browned, stirring to crumble. Drain off pan drippings.

Add remaining ingredients; mix well. Spoon mixture into a 2-quart casserole. Cover and bake at 350° for 1 hour and 10 minutes. Yield: 6 to 8 servings.

## RED BEANS AND HAMBURGER

1 pound dried kidney beans
5 cups water
¼ cup bacon drippings
2 tablespoons Worcestershire sauce
1 teaspoon salt
½ teaspoon pepper
1½ pounds ground chuck
1 medium onion, chopped
1 (10-ounce) can tomatoes and green chiles, undrained
2 teaspoons chili powder

Sort and wash beans; place in a large Dutch oven. Add water, bacon drippings, Worcestershire sauce, salt, and pepper. Bring to a boil. Reduce heat; simmer 10 minutes. Remove from heat; cover and let stand at least 1 hour.

Bring to a boil. Reduce heat; cover and simmer 1 hour.

Brown meat and onion in a large skillet over medium heat; drain well. Add beef mixture, tomatoes and green chiles, and chili powder to bean mixture, mixing well. Cover and simmer 1 hour, stirring occasionally. Yield: 6 servings.

## PICADILLO

1 small onion, finely chopped
1 small green pepper, seeded and chopped
1 clove garlic, minced
2 tablespoons olive oil
2 pounds ground chuck
12 pimiento-stuffed olives, sliced
1 large tomato, peeled, seeded, and chopped
¼ cup tomato sauce
¼ cup water
2 tablespoons capers
1 tablespoon wine vinegar
1 teaspoon salt
1 bay leaf
½ teaspoon dried whole oregano
½ teaspoon brown sugar
4 drops hot sauce
Dash of nutmeg
Hot cooked rice

Sauté onion, green pepper, and garlic in hot oil in a large skillet. Add meat; cook over low heat until meat is browned, stirring to crumble. Drain off pan drippings.

Add remaining ingredients except rice, mixing well. Simmer 5 minutes, uncovered. Cover and simmer 40 minutes. Remove from heat, and discard bay leaf. Serve over hot cooked rice. Yield: 6 servings.

*An entertaining pasta label from the early 1900s.*

## JOHNNIE MARZETTI

1 pound ground chuck
3 stalks celery, chopped
2 medium onions, chopped
1 medium-size green pepper,
 seeded and chopped
¼ cup butter or margarine
1 (6-ounce) can tomato
 paste
1 cup water
¼ teaspoon basil leaves
1 teaspoon salt
¼ teaspoon pepper
1 bay leaf
2 (5-ounce) packages wide egg
 noodles, cooked and
 drained
1½ cups soft breadcrumbs
1 cup (4 ounces) shredded
 sharp Cheddar cheese

Sauté meat, celery, onion, and green pepper in butter in a large skillet over low heat until meat is browned, stirring to crumble. Drain off pan drippings. Add tomato paste, water, basil, salt, pepper, and bay leaf; reduce heat and simmer, uncovered, 5 minutes. Remove bay leaf, and discard.

Place cooked noodles in a lightly greased 2½-quart shallow baking dish. Spoon meat mixture over noodles; sprinkle breadcrumbs and cheese over top. Bake, uncovered, at 375° for 20 minutes or until cheese melts. Yield: 8 to 10 servings.

*Johnnie Marzetti. Spelling varies according to locale, but it is the same hearty, flavorful, economical dish no matter how you spell it.*

## TONY'S ITALIAN PASTA-MEAT PIE

1¼ pounds ground chuck
2 eggs, beaten
½ cup finely grated Romano
 cheese
¼ cup soft breadcrumbs
¼ cup chopped fresh
 parsley
½ teaspoon salt
½ teaspoon pepper
1 cup small star or alphabet
 macaroni
1 cup tomato sauce, divided
1 (8-ounce) can mushroom
 stems and pieces, drained
½ pound bulk pork sausage
2 cups (8 ounces) shredded
 Mozzarella cheese

Combine meat, eggs, Romano cheese, breadcrumbs, parsley, salt, and pepper; mix well. Shape into a ball, and place on a lightly greased 12-inch pizza pan. Press evenly on bottom and sides of pan.

Cook macaroni according to package directions; drain well. Combine macaroni, 2 tablespoons tomato sauce, and mushrooms; spread evenly over meat. Top with remaining tomato sauce.

Brown sausage in a small skillet, stirring to crumble; drain well. Sprinkle sausage evenly over tomato sauce. Top with Mozzarella cheese. Bake at 350° for 20 minutes. Cut into wedges to serve. Yield: 8 servings.

Boeuf Gras

The Pursuit of Pleasure — Tuesday February 21, 1882

Parade of Rex. Monarch

The Historic New Orleans Collection, 533 Royal Street

44

*Bœuf Gras, a New Orleans Mardi Gras scene by Boyd Cruise, 1881.*

## LOUISIANA MEAT PIE

1½ pounds ground chuck
1 small onion, chopped
¼ cup butter or
   margarine
2 tablespoons chopped
   fresh parsley
½ teaspoon salt
½ teaspoon dried whole
   thyme
¼ teaspoon pepper
1 cup beef broth
1 tablespoon all-purpose
   flour
Pastry for double-crust
   9-inch pie

Cook meat in a large skillet over medium heat until browned, stirring occasionally. Drain well, and set aside.

Sauté onion in butter in a large skillet until tender; add cooked meat, parsley, salt, thyme, and pepper, stirring well. Combine beef broth and flour; stir well. Add broth mixture to meat mixture, stirring well. Cook over low heat, stirring frequently, until slightly thickened.

Line a 9-inch pieplate with half of pastry. Pour meat mixture into pastry shell. Cover with top crust. Trim edges of pastry; seal and flute edges. Cut slits in top for steam to escape. Bake at 350° for 1 hour or until crust is golden brown. Yield: 6 to 8 servings.

## BEEF AND PORK PASTIES

¼ pound ground chuck
¼ pound ground pork
½ cup chopped onion
¼ cup chopped celery
1 tablespoon chopped fresh
   parsley
¼ teaspoon salt
⅛ teaspoon dry mustard
⅛ teaspoon rubbed sage
⅛ teaspoon dried whole
   savory
⅛ teaspoon white pepper
½ cup beef broth
¼ cup cooked mashed
   potatoes
¼ cup fine dry breadcrumbs
1 egg, beaten
2 (17¼-ounce) packages
   frozen puff pastry, thawed
1 egg, beaten

Combine meat, onion, and celery in a large skillet; cook until meat is browned, stirring to crumble. Drain off pan drippings. Add next 7 ingredients; reduce heat and simmer, uncovered, 5 minutes. Remove from heat; stir in potatoes, breadcrumbs, and 1 egg. Set aside, and let cool.

Cut each sheet of puff pastry into 4 equal squares. Place 2 tablespoons meat mixture on each square; brush edges of pastry with beaten egg. Fold pastry in half to form triangles; press edges together with tines of fork to seal.

Place on lightly greased baking sheets. Brush tops with beaten egg. Bake at 375° for 25 to 30 minutes or until lightly browned. Yield: 16 turnovers.

Symbolic of Fat Tuesday, portending the onset of Lent, "Bœuf Gras" was a New Orleans tradition dating back to the Middle Ages. The fatted ox had been part of street festivities for years before the pageant of Rex, King of Carnival, began in 1872. In 1901 it was decided that the "Bœuf," attended by cooks and butchers, was not in keeping with the beauty of the rest of the parade, and the practice was stopped. In 1959, Bœuf Gras reappeared in papier mâché on a float in the Mardi Gras parade.

# POLISH MEAT PIES

4 cups all-purpose flour
1 teaspoon salt
4 eggs
⅔ cup water
3 tablespoons chopped onion
2 tablespoons butter or
  margarine
¾ pound ground chuck
½ cup chopped fresh
  mushrooms
3 tablespoons commercial
  sour cream
½ teaspoon salt
Sour Cream Sauce

Sift together flour and salt. Combine eggs and water in a large mixing bowl, beating well. Gradually add flour mixture to egg mixture, stirring well to form a firm dough. Cover and let rest 20 minutes.

Sauté onion in butter in a heavy skillet until tender. Add meat; cook over medium heat until meat is browned, stirring to crumble. Stir in mushrooms, sour cream, and salt; set aside.

Turn dough out onto a lightly floured surface, and divide into 16 equal portions. Shape each portion into a ball. Roll each ball into a 4-inch circle. Place 1 tablespoon meat mixture in center of each circle. Moisten edges of pastry with water; fold pastry in half. Press edges together with fork tines to seal.

Place turnovers, a few at a time, in boiling salted water. Cook 5 minutes; drain on paper towels. Transfer to a 13- x 9- x 2-inch baking dish. Pour Sour Cream Sauce over turnovers; bake at 375° for 20 minutes. Yield: 16 turnovers.

## Sour Cream Sauce:

¼ cup all-purpose flour
2 cups beef broth
1 (8-ounce) carton
  commercial sour cream
1 cup chopped fresh
  mushrooms
½ teaspoon salt

Combine flour and broth in a heavy saucepan, stirring well. Add sour cream, mushrooms and salt; stir well. Cook over low heat, stirring constantly, until thickened and bubbly. Yield: about 3 cups.

# HOT TAMALE PIE

2 pounds ground chuck
1 large onion, chopped
2 cloves garlic, minced
2 (6-ounce) cans tomato paste
1½ cups water
¼ cup chili powder
1 teaspoon salt
2 cups yellow cornmeal
6 cups water, divided
2 teaspoons salt

Combine meat, onion, and garlic in a large skillet; cook over medium heat until meat is browned, stirring to crumble. Drain off pan drippings. Add tomato paste, 1½ cups water, chili powder, and 1 teaspoon salt; reduce heat and simmer, uncovered, 15 minutes or until thickened, stirring occasionally.

Combine cornmeal and 1 cup water in a small bowl, stirring well; set aside. Bring remaining 5 cups water to a boil in a large Dutch oven; stir in 2 teaspoons salt and cornmeal mixture. Simmer, uncovered, 30 minutes, stirring often.

Spread half of cornmeal mixture in bottom of a lightly greased 12- x 8- x 2-inch baking dish. Spoon meat mixture over cornmeal mixture. Spread remaining cornmeal mixture evenly over meat mixture. Bake at 350° for 30 minutes or until firm. Yield: 10 to 12 servings.

*The egg-beating tool of yesteryear depended on people power.*

From bean dip to tortillas, Mexican foods have become so popular that we almost forget the ethnic origin. Tex-Mex staples such as nachos, refried beans, and tamales are eaten by Americans who have never met a Mexican. Restaurants ranging from authentic to ersatz purvey versions of Mexican food to a public becoming more and more discriminating. Easily made at home, Mexican food is delicious and economical.

*Texas women in Mexican costume with baskets and cooking utensils, c.1935.*

## BEEF EMPANADAS

3 medium tomatoes, peeled
  and chopped
½ cup chopped onion
2 tablespoons butter or
  margarine
¾ pound ground chuck
1 teaspoon salt
¼ teaspoon pepper
1 bay leaf
Sweet Potato Pastry
Vegetable oil

Press tomatoes through a sieve. Set tomato puree aside.

Sauté onion in butter in a heavy skillet over low heat until tender. Add meat, salt, pepper, and bay leaf; cook over medium heat until meat is browned, stirring to crumble. Drain off pan drippings. Add tomato puree to meat mixture; cook, uncovered, over low heat 35 minutes. Remove from heat, and discard bay leaf.

Roll pastry to ⅛-inch thickness on a sheet of plastic wrap; cut with a 3½-inch biscuit cutter. Place 1 teaspoon meat mixture in center of each circle. Moisten edges of pastry with water. Fold pastry in half. Press edges together with fork tines to seal. Place turnovers on a baking sheet; cover and refrigerate 2 hours.

Heat 1½ inches of oil to 375° in a large skillet. Cook several turnovers at a time 4 minutes or until golden brown. Drain turnovers on paper towels. Serve hot. Yield: about 2½ dozen.

Sweet Potato Pastry:

3 large sweet potatoes
1½ cups milk
1½ tablespoons firmly packed
  brown sugar
2¼ teaspoons salt
3 cups Masa Harina (instant
  corn tortilla mix)

Place sweet potatoes in a medium saucepan with water to cover. Bring to a boil. Cover and cook 20 minutes or until tender; drain. Let cool to the touch; peel and mash.

Combine mashed sweet potatoes, milk, sugar, and salt; beat well. Stir in Masa Harina, mixing until well blended. Turn dough out onto a lightly floured surface; knead 5 minutes. Divide dough in half, and cover with plastic wrap. Yield: enough pastry for 2½ dozen turnovers.

*A botanical print of corn.*

## HOT TAMALES

2 to 2½ dozen dried corn
  husks
½ pound bulk pork sausage
1 pound ground chuck
3 tablespoons chili powder
1 tablespoon salt
4 cups yellow cornmeal
1½ teaspoons salt
¾ cup shortening
1¾ cups boiling water

Place corn husks in a large container; cover with hot water. Let stand 1 to 2 hours or until softened. Drain well; pat dry.

Combine meat, chili powder, and 1 tablespoon salt; mix well.

Combine cornmeal, 1½ teaspoons salt, shortening, and boiling water in a large mixing bowl; stir until shortening melts and mixture is well blended.

Place 2 tablespoons cornmeal mixture down center of each husk; spread to within ½ inch of edge. Place 2 tablespoons meat mixture on cornmeal, spreading evenly. Fold sides of husk to center, enclosing filling completely. Fold pointed end under; tie with string or strips of corn husk. (If husks are too narrow, overlap 2 husks to make a wide one. If husks are too wide, tear off one side.)

Layer tamales in a large Dutch oven; add water to cover. Bring to a boil; cover and simmer 40 minutes. Drain well. Serve tamales in husks. Remove husks before eating. Yield: about 2 dozen.

## TEXAS ENCHILADAS

2 pounds ground chuck
1 medium onion, chopped
1 medium-size green pepper,
  seeded and chopped
1 tablespoon garlic powder
1 tablespoon chili powder
1 teaspoon salt
½ teaspoon pepper
½ teaspoon ground cumin
3 tablespoons picante sauce
⅛ teaspoon hot sauce
½ cup chopped ripe olives
1½ dozen frozen corn
  tortillas, thawed
Vegetable oil
½ cup butter or margarine
¼ cup all-purpose flour
1½ cups milk
1 (16-ounce) carton
  commercial sour cream
2 cups (8 ounces) shredded
  sharp Cheddar cheese
Sliced ripe olives (optional)

Cook meat in a large skillet over medium heat until browned, stirring to crumble; drain well. Add onion and green pepper; cover and simmer 10 minutes or until vegetables are tender. Add garlic powder, chili powder, salt, pepper, cumin, picante sauce, hot sauce, and chopped olives; cover and simmer 5 minutes. Remove from heat, and set aside.

Fry tortillas, one at a time, in ¼ inch hot oil (375°) for 5 seconds on each side or just until softened. Drain tortillas on paper towels. Spoon meat mixture evenly in center of each tortilla, and roll up. Place tortillas, seam side down, in a lightly greased jellyroll pan. Set aside.

Melt butter in a heavy saucepan over low heat; add flour and cook 1 minute, stirring constantly. Gradually add milk; cook over medium heat, stirring constantly, until sauce is thickened and bubbly. Add sour cream, and cook 1 minute or until thoroughly heated.

Pour sour cream sauce evenly over enchiladas; sprinkle with cheese. Bake at 350° for 20 minutes or until bubbly. Top with sliced ripe olives, if desired. Yield: 18 enchiladas.

## TACOS

2½ pounds ground chuck
4 cloves garlic, minced
1 tablespoon chili powder
1 teaspoon salt
½ teaspoon pepper
1 small head iceberg lettuce,
  shredded
3 tomatoes, peeled and
  chopped
¼ cup chopped onion
3 (8-ounce) packages frozen
  corn tortillas, thawed
Vegetable oil
2 cups (8 ounces) shredded
  Cheddar cheese
Hot sauce (recipe follows)

Combine meat, garlic, chili powder, salt, and pepper in a large skillet; cook over medium heat until meat is browned, stirring to crumble.

Combine lettuce, tomatoes, and onion in a large mixing bowl; set aside.

Fry tortillas in deep hot oil (375°) until crisp, folding in middle to form taco shell. Drain on paper towels.

Fill each taco shell with 2 tablespoons meat mixture; top with lettuce mixture and cheese. Serve with hot sauce. Yield: 24 tacos.

### Hot Sauce:

3 medium tomatoes, peeled
  and chopped
1 (3-ounce) can chopped
  green chiles, drained
2 cloves garlic
1 tablespoon vinegar
1 tablespoon olive oil
1 teaspoon salt
½ teaspoon pepper

Combine all ingredients in container of an electric blender; process on medium speed until smooth. Store in an airtight container in refrigerator. Yield: about 2½ cups.

*Hot Tamales (rear), Tacos, and Sour Cream Enchiladas. Popularity of Tex-Mex food has spread, but the closer one is to the Southwest, the better the food is apt to be.*

*Rice's seeds bring hefty returns, c.1890.*

## STUFFED CABBAGE ROLLS

1 (15-ounce) can tomato sauce, divided
2 medium potatoes, cubed
2 large onions, cubed
2 eggs
3 cloves garlic
2 teaspoons salt
1 teaspoon pepper
2½ pounds ground chuck
3 large heads of cabbage
2 (14½-ounce) cans whole tomatoes, undrained
1 (28-ounce) jar apple butter
½ cup lemon juice
2 large onions, chopped
1 tablespoon sugar
1 tablespoon firmly packed brown sugar
2 teaspoons salt

Combine 3 tablespoons tomato sauce, potatoes, cubed onion, eggs, garlic, salt, and pepper in container of an electric blender. Process until well blended. Combine tomato mixture and meat in a large mixing bowl; mix well. Set aside.

Core cabbage, and set aside. Place heads in hot water to cover until leaves are easily separated. Remove leaves. Cook leaves in boiling salted water 5 to 8 minutes or until just tender; drain. Place about ¼ cup meat mixture in center of each cabbage leaf; fold ends over, and tie with string. Shred remaining cabbage; place in bottom of a large Dutch oven. Place cabbage rolls on shredded cabbage.

Combine remaining ingredients; mix well. Pour over cabbage rolls. Cover; simmer 2 hours. Remove rolls; serve with sauce. Yield: 12 to 14 servings.

## COUNTRY BEEF SAUSAGE

5 pounds ground chuck
3 tablespoons rubbed sage
1 tablespoon plus 1 teaspoon red pepper flakes
1 tablespoon salt
½ teaspoon red pepper

Combine all ingredients in a large mixing bowl, mixing well. Cover and refrigerate overnight. Shape mixture into five 1-pound rolls; wrap tightly in plastic wrap. Chill thoroughly.

Slice sausage to desired thickness. Place slices in a skillet over medium heat; cook 4 minutes on each side or until desired degree of doneness. Yield: five 1-pound rolls.

*Note*: Sausage rolls may be wrapped in aluminum foil and frozen. Thaw in refrigerator before slicing and frying.

## BEEF-STUFFED GREEN PEPPERS

4 medium-size green peppers
1 medium onion, chopped
1 clove garlic, minced
2 tablespoons butter or margarine
½ pound ground chuck
1 (14½-ounce) can tomatoes, drained and chopped
¾ cup cooked regular rice
1 teaspoon salt
⅛ teaspoon pepper
⅓ cup shredded Cheddar cheese
⅓ cup buttered cracker crumbs

Cut off tops and remove seeds from peppers. Discard seeds and set tops aside. Cook peppers 5 minutes in boiling salted water; drain well, and set aside.

Chop tops of peppers; combine with onion and garlic. Sauté vegetables in butter in a large skillet until tender; add meat, and cook until meat is browned, stirring to crumble. Drain well. Stir in tomatoes, rice, salt, and pepper.

Fill peppers with meat mixture. Place in an 8-inch square baking dish. Top each pepper with cheese and cracker crumbs. Bake at 350° for 25 to 30 minutes. Yield: 4 servings.

*Butcher's sign shows tools of the trade, c.1889.*

Index of American Design, National Gallery of Art

# BEEF IN COMBINATION

## ALABAMA CHILI

2½ pounds boneless chuck
  roast, cut into ½-inch
  cubes
¼ cup olive oil
¼ cup all-purpose flour
2 tablespoons chili powder
5 cloves garlic, minced
1 teaspoon ground cumin
1 teaspoon ground
  oregano
2 cups beef broth
1 teaspoon salt
½ teaspoon coarsely ground
  black pepper
Pinto Beans

Brown meat in olive oil in a
large Dutch oven over medium
heat. Combine flour and chili
powder; mix well. Sprinkle flour
mixture over meat, stirring to
coat well. Add minced garlic,
cumin, oregano, beef broth,
salt, and pepper. Bring mixture
to a boil. Reduce heat; cover and
simmer 4 hours, stirring occasionally. Serve chili over Pinto
Beans. Yield: 6 servings.

Pinto Beans:

½ pound dried pinto beans
¼ pound salt pork
1 medium onion, chopped
1 teaspoon salt

Sort and wash beans; place in
a medium saucepan. Cover with
water, and soak overnight.
Drain beans. Return beans to
saucepan; add pork, onion, salt,
and water to cover. Bring to a
boil; reduce heat. Cover and
cook 30 minutes or until beans
are tender. Yield: 6 servings.

*Mexican officer at Gebhardt Chili Co., San Antonio.*

## PEDERNALES RIVER CHILI

4 pounds coarsely ground
  chuck
1 large onion, chopped
2 cloves garlic, minced
1 (28-ounce) can whole
  tomatoes, undrained and
  chopped
2 cups water
2 tablespoons chili powder
2 teaspoons salt
1 teaspoon ground oregano
1 teaspoon ground cumin

Combine meat, onion, and
garlic in a large Dutch oven;
cook over medium heat until
meat is browned, stirring to
crumble. Drain off pan drippings. Add remaining ingredients, mixing well. Cover and
simmer 1 hour, stirring occasionally. Yield: about 12 cups.

**W**illiam Gebhardt was
granted the "Eagle
Brand" registration
for his chili powder in 1896;
it was to become one of the
oldest continuous trade-
marks in the country. Gebhardt operated a café in New
Braunfels, Texas, until the
1890s, when, finding his
Mexican food out-selling his
German dishes, he moved to
San Antonio. He is regarded
as the father of the Mexican
food industry, having been
the first to grind and blend
the ancho chile pepper with
black pepper, comino
(cumin), oregano, and garlic
to make "chili powder."

# SMALL RED CHILI PEPPER

## ORIGINAL TEXAS-STYLE BOWL OF RED

4 dried hot chile peppers, seeded
3 pounds lean beef for stewing, cut into 1½-inch cubes
2 tablespoons vegetable oil
4 cups water
2 cloves garlic, minced
1 tablespoon salt
1 tablespoon ground oregano
1 tablespoon ground cumin
1 tablespoon red pepper
1 tablespoon chili powder
1 tablespoon hot sauce
2½ tablespoons Masa Harina (instant corn tortilla mix)

Place hot peppers in a small amount of water in a small saucepan. Bring to a boil. Reduce heat, and simmer 30 minutes. Drain well. Finely chop peppers, and set aside.

Brown meat in oil over medium heat in a large Dutch oven. Drain well. Add chopped peppers and water. Bring to a boil. Reduce heat, and simmer 30 minutes.

Add garlic, salt, oregano, cumin, red pepper, chili powder, and hot sauce; bring to a boil. Reduce heat, and simmer 1 hour and 30 minutes. Add Masa Harina, stirring well. Cover and cook over low heat 30 minutes. Yield: about 7 cups.

*Original Texas-Style Bowl of Red is the definitive article revered by purists. Meat is cut, not ground, and it contains no beans or onions. Just spices.*

exas has always had room for heroes, and when the subject of chili comes up, the name that arises is that of Francis X. Tolbert. No, this fourth-generation Texan, who was a former columnist for the *Dallas Morning News* and author of numerous books, didn't invent the stuff; neither do we know who invented the wheel. But we're pretty sure that it was Tolbert's missionary zeal that put chili within the reach and the cast-iron stomachs of people around the world.

It was Tolbert who organized the Chili Appreciation Society and co-founded the annual Chili Cookoff at Terlingua, Texas. His definitive book on chili, *A Bowl of Red*, 1966, has been reissued in paperback so that another generation may learn the true and fiery path to chili Heaven, where no vegetable may enter save the chile pepper. In this witty treatise on the subject of chili, Tolbert recounted that when the West was young, chili was a staple on jailhouse menus. Villains, it was said, planned to stage their most daring escapades in or near towns whose jail cooks had the best reputations for making chili. The theory was that in case a particular crime did not pay, at least the food would be good during the lull while plans were laid for the next felony.

*Francis X. Tolbert, 1981*

Photographer: Clint Grant

*Brisket Stew for a lusty one-dish meal.*

## BRISKET STEW

1 cup all-purpose flour
1 teaspoon salt
½ teaspoon pepper
3 pounds brisket, cut into cubes
2 tablespoons vegetable oil
1 quart water
2 small onions, chopped
2 cloves garlic, minced
1 teaspoon salt
½ teaspoon pepper
12 small red potatoes, peeled
12 baby carrots, scraped
10 small onions, peeled

Combine flour, 1 teaspoon salt, and ½ teaspoon pepper in a plastic or paper bag; shake to mix. Place brisket cubes, a few at a time, in bag; shake well.

Cook brisket cubes in hot oil in a large Dutch oven over medium heat, stirring to brown on all sides. Add water, chopped onion, garlic, salt, and pepper. Cover and simmer 1 hour. Add remaining ingredients. Cover and simmer 1 hour and 15 minutes or until vegetables are tender. Yield: 8 cups.

## OLD-FASHIONED BEEF STEW

3 pounds lean beef for stewing, cut into 1-inch cubes
3 tablespoons bacon drippings
2 (14½-ounce) cans whole tomatoes, undrained
2 (15½-ounce) cans tomato sauce
12 carrots, peeled and cut into ½-inch slices
2 large potatoes, cubed
2 large onions, cubed
1 teaspoon salt
1 teaspoon lemon pepper
1 teaspoon celery salt
1 tablespoon Italian herb seasoning
1 tablespoon Worcestershire sauce
1 large green pepper, coarsely chopped
2 (10-ounce) packages frozen green peas
¼ cup cooking sherry

Brown meat in bacon drippings in a large Dutch oven over medium heat. Stir in next 10 ingredients; mix well, and bring to a boil. Reduce heat; cover and simmer over low heat 1 hour and 40 minutes or until meat and vegetables are tender. Add green pepper, peas, and sherry. Cover and cook an additional 15 minutes. Yield: 5 quarts.

## BEEF RAGÔUT

7 slices bacon
1 pound boneless round steak, cut into 2-inch pieces
1 teaspoon salt
¼ teaspoon pepper
3 medium onions, sliced
2 medium carrots, scraped and cut into ½-inch pieces
4 medium potatoes, peeled and thinly sliced
1 cup water

Cook bacon in a large Dutch oven until crisp; remove bacon, reserving drippings for use in another recipe. Crumble bacon, and set aside.

Layer steak and crumbled bacon in Dutch oven. Sprinkle salt and pepper over top. Arrange onions, carrots, and potatoes over steak; add water. Bring mixture to a boil. Reduce heat; cover and simmer 45 minutes. Yield: about 8 cups.

# DEEP-DISH BEEF PIE

1 pound round steak, cubed
1 medium onion, chopped
3 potatoes, peeled and diced
1 teaspoon salt
¼ teaspoon pepper
1 tablespoon all-purpose flour
¼ cup water
Pastry for deep-dish
    double-crust 9-inch pie

Place meat, onion, and potatoes in a small Dutch oven; add water to cover. Bring to a boil. Reduce heat; cover and simmer until vegetables are tender. Add salt and pepper.

Combine flour and water; stir until smooth. Gradually add to meat mixture; cook over medium heat until thickened and bubbly. Cool and set aside.

Roll half of pastry to ⅛-inch thickness on a lightly floured surface; fit into a deep 9-inch pieplate. Pour meat mixture into pastry shell. Roll out remaining pastry to ⅛-inch thickness; place over filling. Trim edges; seal and flute. Cut slits in top to allow steam to escape. Bake at 350° for 45 minutes or until golden brown. Yield: one 9-inch pie.

PRIDE OF AMERICA.

MAMMOTH PEARL.

SNOWFLAKE.

# STEW FROM SUNDAY'S ROAST

4 carrots, scraped and sliced
2 large potatoes, peeled and cubed
2 medium onions, chopped
3 to 4 cups cooked, cubed roast beef
1 (14½-ounce) can tomatoes, undrained and chopped
1 (8¾-ounce) can whole kernel corn
1 (8½-ounce) can green peas
1 cup shredded cabbage
½ cup catsup
1 teaspoon salt
½ teaspoon pepper
½ teaspoon celery salt

Combine carrots, potatoes, onion, and water to cover in a large Dutch oven. Bring to a boil. Reduce heat; simmer 10 minutes. Stir in remaining ingredients. Simmer 45 minutes. Yield: 8 cups.

# OLD-FASHIONED CHOPPED SOUTHERN BEEF HASH

4 cups cooked, chopped roast beef
3 medium onions, chopped
3 tablespoons butter or margarine
4 medium potatoes, peeled and cubed
3 cups beef broth
1 tablespoon Worcestershire sauce
½ teaspoon salt
¼ teaspoon pepper
Hot biscuits

Sauté meat and onion in butter in a large Dutch oven over low heat 5 minutes, stirring occasionally. Add remaining ingredients, except biscuits; simmer, uncovered, 30 minutes or until potatoes are tender. Serve over hot biscuits. Yield: 8 to 10 servings.

*A lesson in making pastry for meat pies is in progress.*

*A fine figure of a bull surveys his pasture.*

## BEEF HASH WITH INDIAN GRIDDLE CAKES

¼ cup butter or margarine
¼ cup all-purpose flour
2 cups beef broth
½ cup chopped onion
¼ teaspoon Worcestershire sauce
Salt and pepper to taste
Pinch of red pepper
4 cups cooked, chopped roast beef
Indian Griddle Cakes

Melt butter in a large, heavy saucepan over low heat; add flour, stirring until smooth. Cook 1 minute, stirring constantly. Gradually add beef broth; cook over medium heat, stirring constantly until thickened and bubbly. Add next 5 ingredients, mixing well. Serve hot over Indian Griddle Cakes. Yield: 6 servings.

### Indian Griddle Cakes:

1 cup plus 2 tablespoons cornmeal
½ cup all-purpose flour
1 tablespoon sugar
½ teaspoon salt
½ teaspoon baking soda
½ teaspoon baking powder
1 egg
1 cup buttermilk
2 tablespoons vegetable oil
½ cup milk

Combine dry ingredients in a medium mixing bowl; set aside. Combine egg, buttermilk, and oil; slowly stir into dry ingredients. Add milk to desired consistency, mixing lightly.

Pour batter by ¼ cupfuls onto a hot, lightly greased griddle. Turn pancakes when tops are covered with bubbles and edges are browned. Serve griddle cakes hot with Beef Hash. Yield: about 12 pancakes.

## BEEF POT PIE

1 large onion, chopped
3 tablespoons butter or margarine
2 cups cooked, cubed roast beef
1 tablespoon all-purpose flour
1 cup beef broth
1 cup diced, cooked potatoes
1 cup cooked green peas and carrots
2 tablespoons chopped fresh parsley
2 tablespoons sherry
1 teaspoon Worcestershire sauce
½ teaspoon salt
½ teaspoon pepper
⅛ teaspoon dried whole thyme
Pastry for 9-inch pie
1 egg, beaten

Sauté onion in butter until tender. Add meat; cook 5 minutes. Sprinkle flour over meat, stirring constantly. Gradually add broth; cook over medium heat, stirring constantly, until thickened. Stir in next 8 ingredients. Spoon mixture into a 9-inch pieplate.

Roll pastry to ⅛-inch thickness on a lightly floured surface. Carefully place pastry over beef mixture. Turn pastry edges under, and press firmly to rim of pieplate to seal; flute edges. Cut slits in top to allow steam to escape. Decorate with pastry cutouts, if desired. Brush top with beaten egg. Bake at 350° for 45 minutes or until golden brown. Yield: 6 servings.

*Beef Pot Pie. With meat and vegetables tucked under pastry, dinner needs only salad and dessert to be completely satisfying.*

*Refrigerated shipping revolutionized meat distribution.*

## ROAST BEEF ROLLS

1 cup soft breadcrumbs
2 tablespoons finely chopped onion
¼ teaspoon poultry seasoning
¼ teaspoon salt
⅛ teaspoon pepper
⅛ teaspoon paprika
4 (8- x 4- x ⅛-inch) slices cooked roast beef
¼ cup all-purpose flour
2 tablespoons vegetable oil
1 cup milk
½ teaspoon salt
¼ teaspoon pepper
4 slices toasted bread

Combine breadcrumbs, onion, seasoning, ¼ teaspoon salt, ⅛ teaspoon pepper, and paprika; mix well. Spoon one-fourth mixture on each beef slice. Roll up jellyroll fashion; secure with wooden picks.

Dredge beef rolls in flour; reserve 2 tablespoons flour for gravy. Brown beef rolls in hot oil in a large skillet over medium heat. Remove beef rolls from skillet. Stir in reserved flour. Cook 1 minute, stirring constantly. Gradually add milk; cook over medium heat, stirring constantly, until thickened and bubbly. Stir in salt and pepper.

Place beef rolls in skillet with gravy. Cover and cook over low heat 15 minutes. Serve beef rolls and gravy over toasted bread. Yield: 4 servings.

## SLUMGULLION

3 cups cooked, cubed roast beef
2 cups beef broth
1 (14½-ounce) can tomatoes, drained and chopped
1 tablespoon Worcestershire sauce
½ teaspoon salt
½ teaspoon pepper
2 medium onions, chopped
½ cup uncooked regular rice
2 tablespoons butter or margarine

Combine first 6 ingredients in a medium Dutch oven; simmer 10 minutes.

Sauté onion and rice in butter in a heavy skillet until onion is tender. Stir onion mixture into beef mixture. Pour into a lightly greased 2-quart casserole. Cover and bake at 350° for 40 minutes. Yield: 6 to 8 servings.

## JELLIED LOAF OF BEEF

2 hard-cooked eggs, sliced
3 envelopes unflavored gelatin
3 cups hot beef broth
4½ cups chopped, cooked roast beef
½ cup finely chopped onion
½ cup finely chopped celery
½ cup finely chopped green pepper
1 teaspoon salt
½ teaspoon pepper
½ teaspoon hot sauce
Lettuce leaves (optional)

Line a lightly oiled 9- x 5- x 3-inch loafpan with sliced eggs, and set aside.

Combine gelatin and beef broth in a large mixing bowl, stirring until gelatin is dissolved. Stir in roast beef, onion, celery, green pepper, salt, pepper, and hot sauce; spoon mixture into prepared loafpan. Cover and chill overnight.

To serve, unmold onto lettuce-lined platter and slice. Yield: 1 (9-inch) loaf.

# VEAL

## Delicate in Taste, Always a Festive Dish

---

Veal to be at its best is slaughtered when six to eight weeks old, at weaning time, before the animal begins to eat grass. Once the calf is turned out to graze, the flesh darkens and it is no longer veal; it is young beef. Veal less than a month old is called "Bob" veal, and is, to most minds, too underdeveloped to be good eating.

When the colonists were struggling to gain a foothold on the East Coast, one of their hardest problems was feeding their meat animals through the winter. Often, rather than winter beef cattle over, they simply slaughtered them as veal, sacrificing meat poundage in favor of tenderness. The animal, when mature, was scrawny and sinewy in the extreme.

Veal, like any other immature meat animal, is quite dry and needs to be cooked with fat added, many times in the form of larding. Larding is the introduction of strips of fat pork by way of a "needle" bought for the purpose. Laced through with fat, a chunk of veal can be a dish fit for kings. Veal is never broiled or seared; it simply loses what moisture is in it when so treated.

Breast of veal must be confronted with all due caution. It is short on meat and long on gristle and bone. Our grandmothers had no choice but to use it; it was, after all, food. But we with our sophisticated butchers' shops can opt for cuts with more edible meat per pound of bought weight. The butcher sells veal riblets, veal stew meat, and ground veal for mock chicken legs and loaves. If we avail ourselves of these versions of veal breast, we carry home less gristle and bone.

The blandness of veal is a plus in that it is amenable to seasonings, either subtle or stimulating. Our European forebears knew how to treat veal: From Vienna we have wiener schnitzel; from Italy the scallopinis, marsala and piccata; from Hungary, paprika; from France a lovely provençal . . . all toothsome morsels. Veal, if carefully done, can taste as expensive as it is.

*Veal Cutlets Provençal (page 73). Tomatoes and mushrooms are implicit in the term provençal, and there is always a hint of garlic as well.*

# ROASTS FIT FOR A KING

## MARINATED VEAL ROAST

2 slices bacon, finely chopped
1 large onion, chopped
½ cup olive oil
½ cup lemon juice
1 clove garlic, minced
¼ cup chopped fresh parsley
1 teaspoon marjoram leaves
1 teaspoon dried whole thyme
½ teaspoon caraway seeds
½ teaspoon salt
¼ teaspoon white pepper
1 (5½- to 6-pound) rolled veal leg roast
2 cups water

Combine bacon, onion, olive oil, lemon juice, garlic, parsley, marjoram, thyme, caraway seeds, salt, and pepper in a small mixing bowl; mix well. Set aside for 30 minutes.

Place roast in a well-greased shallow roasting pan. Pour marinade over roast; cover and refrigerate 24 hours, turning occasionally.

Insert meat thermometer, if desired. Stir water into marinade mixture. Bake, uncovered, at 300° for 3½ hours or until meat thermometer registers 170° (well done), basting occasionally with pan drippings.

Transfer roast to a warm serving platter. Serve the pan drippings as a gravy. Yield: 12 servings.

## OVEN-ROASTED VEAL WITH NEW POTATOES

¼ cup plus 2 tablespoons all-purpose flour, divided
1½ teaspoons salt
⅛ teaspoon pepper
1 (4- to 4½-pound) rolled veal rump roast, unrolled
6 slices bacon
10 new potatoes, peeled
1 cup water

Combine 2 tablespoons flour, salt, and pepper; mix well. Sprinkle flour mixture evenly over roast, coating well. Arrange bacon slices over top of roast, securing with wooden picks.

Place veal on a well-greased rack in a covered roasting pan. Insert meat thermometer, if desired. Cover and bake at 300° for 2 hours. Add potatoes, and continue baking, uncovered, for 25 minutes or until meat thermometer registers 170° (well done).

Transfer roast to a large serving platter. Let stand 10 minutes before slicing. Return potatoes to oven; place 7 to 8 inches from heating element. Broil 5 minutes or until crusty brown. Arrange browned potatoes on platter with roast.

Pour pan drippings into a small saucepan; set aside. Combine remaining ¼ cup flour and water, mixing well to form a paste. Gradually stir flour mixture into reserved pan drippings. Cook over medium heat, stirring constantly, until thickened and bubbly. Serve gravy with roast and potatoes. Yield: 8 to 10 servings.

## SAVORY ROLLED ROAST OF VEAL

½ cup butter or margarine, melted
2 small onions, finely chopped
2 cloves garlic, minced
¼ cup chopped fresh parsley
2 teaspoons salt
1 teaspoon pepper
1 (3½- to 4-pound) rolled veal rump roast, unrolled
2 tablespoons butter or margarine, melted
1 cup dry white wine
1 (8-ounce) carton commercial sour cream

Combine ½ cup melted butter, onion, garlic, parsley, salt, and pepper; mix well. Spoon one-half of mixture onto roast, spreading to within 2 inches of edge. Roll up jellyroll fashion, enclosing the stuffing completely. Tie roast securely with string. Cover outside of roast with remaining onion mixture.

Place roast in a well-greased shallow roasting pan. Insert meat thermometer, if desired. Pour 2 tablespoons melted butter over roast. Bake, uncovered, at 450° for 15 minutes. Add wine. Reduce heat to 325°, and bake an additional 1½ hours or until meat thermometer registers 170° (well done), basting occasionally. Transfer roast to a serving platter; remove string. Let stand 10 minutes before slicing. Reserve pan drippings.

Remove excess grease from pan drippings, and discard. Strain pan drippings into a medium saucepan. Bring mixture to a boil; reduce heat, and cook over medium heat 30 minutes or until mixture is reduced to 1½ cups. Add sour cream, stirring until well blended. Slice roast, and serve with gravy. Yield: 8 to 10 servings.

*Savory Rolled Roast of Veal, surrounded by baked tomato halves topped with herbed breadcrumbs.*

## VEAL ROAST WITH RICE STUFFING

1 (4-pound) veal top round
  roast, 3 to 4 inches thick,
  butterflied
1 teaspoon salt
⅛ teaspoon pepper
Rice Stuffing
5 slices bacon

Spread roast open, and pound with a meat mallet to 1½- to 2-inch thickness. Season roast on all sides with salt and pepper. Spoon Rice Stuffing onto roast, spreading to within 2 inches of edge. Roll up jellyroll fashion, enclosing the stuffing completely. Tie roast securely with string. Wrap bacon slices around rolled roast; secure with wooden picks.

Place roast on a well-greased rack in a shallow roasting pan. Insert meat thermometer, if desired. Bake, uncovered, at 300° for 2 hours and 35 minutes or until meat thermometer registers 170° (well done).

Transfer roast to a serving platter; remove string. Let stand 10 minutes before slicing. Yield: 8 servings.

Rice Stuffing:

2 tablespoons finely
  chopped onion
2 tablespoons shortening,
  melted
¾ cup uncooked regular
  rice
2 cups beef broth
1 teaspoon salt
1 teaspoon poultry
  seasoning
1 egg, slightly beaten
1 (4-ounce) can stems and
  pieces mushrooms, drained

Sauté onion in shortening in a large skillet over medium heat until tender. Add rice, and cook 5 minutes or until rice is golden brown, stirring occasionally. Add beef broth, salt, and poultry seasoning; stir well.

Cover and cook over low heat 35 minutes or until all liquid is absorbed. Remove from heat; add egg and mushrooms, stirring until well blended. Yield: about 3 cups.

*The sharper the knife, the better the roast.*

## LOUISIANA ROLLED VEAL ROAST

1 (4- to 5-pound) veal rump
  roast, butterflied
1 teaspoon salt
1 teaspoon pepper
1 tablespoon olive oil
½ cup finely chopped onion
2 cloves garlic, minced
¼ teaspoon hot sauce
¼ cup olive oil
2 cups sliced fresh
  mushrooms
1 cup finely chopped, cooked
  ham
2 cups soft breadcrumbs
¼ cup milk
⅛ teaspoon dried whole
  marjoram
⅛ teaspoon dried whole
  thyme
1 teaspoon all-purpose flour
2 cups beef broth
1 cup rosé wine
½ cup finely chopped onion
½ cup finely chopped celery
½ cup finely chopped green
  pepper
2 bay leaves
3 tablespoons all-purpose
  flour
Lemon slices

Spread roast open; pound to 1-inch thickness with a meat mallet.

Sprinkle salt and pepper over entire surface of roast; rub with 1 tablespoon olive oil.

Sauté ½ cup onion, garlic, and hot sauce in ¼ cup olive oil in a large skillet until onion is tender. Add mushrooms and ham; cook 5 minutes. Remove from heat. Add breadcrumbs and milk; mix well.

Place stuffing mixture on roast, leaving a ½-inch margin. Roll up jellyroll fashion, enclosing the stuffing completely. Tie securely with string. Sprinkle roast with marjoram, thyme, and 1 teaspoon flour.

Place in a well-greased shallow roasting pan. Insert meat thermometer, if desired. Bake at 500° for 25 minutes or until roast is browned.

Combine broth, wine, ½ cup onion, celery, green pepper, and bay leaves, mixing well. Reduce heat to 375°. Pour gravy mixture over roast, and bake 45 minutes or until meat thermometer registers 170° (well done), basting occasionally. Transfer roast to a serving platter; remove string. Let stand 10 minutes before slicing. Reserve pan drippings.

Combine 3 tablespoons flour and a small amount of water to form a smooth paste. Stir into pan drippings. Cook over medium heat, stirring constantly, until thickened and bubbly. Remove bay leaves; discard. Slice roast, and serve with gravy. Garnish with lemon slices. Yield: 8 to 10 servings.

# STUFFED VEAL ROAST

1 (4- to 5-pound) veal top round roast, 3 to 4 inches thick, butterflied
1 clove garlic, minced
½ teaspoon ground ginger
½ teaspoon salt
⅛ teaspoon pepper
Dressing (recipe follows)
¼ cup rendered chicken fat
2 tablespoons finely chopped celery
2 tablespoons finely chopped carrot
2 tablespoons finely chopped green pepper
2 tablespoons finely chopped tomato
2 tablespoons finely chopped onion
1 teaspoon lemon juice
1 bay leaf
1 cup water
Brown Gravy

Spread roast open, and pound with a meat mallet to 1½- to 2-inch thickness. Season roast on all sides with garlic, ginger, salt, and pepper. Spoon dressing onto roast, spreading to within 2 inches of edge. Roll up jellyroll fashion, enclosing the stuffing completely. Tie roast securely with string. Make several slits on outside of roast, and stuff with chicken fat.

Place roast in a well-greased, covered roasting pan. Combine celery, carrot, green pepper, tomato, onion, lemon juice, bay leaf, and water. Pour vegetable mixture around roast. Cover and bake at 300° for 2 hours or until meat thermometer registers 170° (well done).

Transfer roast to a serving platter; remove string. Discard bay leaf, and reserve pan drippings for gravy. Let roast stand 10 minutes. Cut into ¼-inch-thick slices, and serve with Brown Gravy. Yield: 8 servings.

*A French Quarter chef in conversation with a customer in a New Orleans restaurant, c.1890.*

Dressing:

3 slices bread, cut into ¼-inch cubes
½ cup water
1 small onion, finely chopped
3 tablespoons rendered chicken fat
½ cup finely chopped celery
2 eggs, beaten
2 saltine crackers, finely crushed
1 tablespoon chopped fresh parsley
½ teaspoon salt
⅛ teaspoon pepper
Dash of ground ginger

Combine bread cubes and water; soak for 10 minutes. Drain well, squeezing out excess water. Discard water, and set bread aside.

Sauté onion in chicken fat in a large skillet over low heat until tender. Add bread and remaining ingredients, stirring well. Yield: about 4 cups.

Brown Gravy:

¼ cup butter or margarine
¼ cup all-purpose flour
2½ cups reserved pan drippings

Melt butter in a medium saucepan; add flour, and cook over medium heat, stirring constantly, 10 minutes or until roux is the color of a copper penny. Gradually stir in pan drippings. Bring to a boil; reduce heat, and simmer 15 minutes. Strain gravy into serving bowl. Yield: about 2½ cups.

The Historic New Orleans Collection, 533 Royal Street

*Tempting Stuffed Veal Roast with Dauphine Potatoes*

## STUFFED VEAL ROAST WITH DAUPHINE POTATOES

1 (2-pound) boneless veal
    sirloin tip roast, butterflied
1½ teaspoons salt, divided
¾ teaspoon pepper, divided
1 pound ground pork
2 tablespoons chopped
    fresh parsley
1 egg, beaten
2 tablespoons fine dry
    breadcrumbs
1 tablespoon cognac
4 slices bacon
¼ cup butter or margarine
Dauphine Potatoes

Spread roast open; pound to
½-inch thickness with a meat
mallet. Sprinkle evenly with 1
teaspoon salt and ½ teaspoon
pepper.

Combine pork, parsley, egg,

dry breadcrumbs, cognac, and
remaining salt and pepper.
Spread stuffing mixture on
roast, leaving a ½-inch margin.
Roll up roast jellyroll fashion.
Wrap bacon in 4 strips around
roast, and tie roll securely with
string. Insert meat thermometer, if desired.

Place roast on a rack in a
roasting pan. Dot with butter.
Cover and bake at 300° for 1
hour. Uncover and bake 1½
hours or until meat thermometer registers 170° (well done).
Transfer roast to a serving platter. Strain pan drippings into a
serving bowl. Place Dauphine
Potatoes around roast; serve
roast and potatoes with gravy.
Yield: 8 servings.

Dauphine Potatoes:

2 pounds potatoes
2 eggs
1 cup (4 ounces) shredded
    sharp Cheddar cheese
2 tablespoons all-purpose
    flour
1 teaspoon salt
Vegetable oil

Cook potatoes in boiling
salted water to cover 20 minutes
or until tender. Cool slightly.
Peel and mash. Add eggs,
cheese, flour, and salt; mix well.

With floured hands, shape po-
tato mixture into 1½-inch balls.
Deep fry in hot oil (375°) until
potatoes are golden brown.
Drain well on paper towels.
Yield: 18 (1½-inch) potatoes.

Fricandeau of veal, one of Jefferson's pets, was a popular nineteenth-century dish, according to the cookbooks of the day, and is still deliciously current. Mrs. Randolph spelled it fricando in 1860; Mrs. Henderson spelled it correctly in her 1877 cookbook.

The recipes are also dissimilar, Henderson's braise with vegetables being closer to Jefferson's method, with tomato sauce recommended. Randolph's recipe, simpler and involving no vegetables, was served surrounded by sorrel that had been stewed with butter, pepper, and salt until it was quite dry.

## VEAL POT ROAST

1 (6- to 7-pound) boneless
  veal rump roast
2 cloves garlic, sliced
6 whole cloves
½ cup butter or margarine
1 (14½-ounce) can whole
  tomatoes, undrained and
  chopped
1 (8-ounce) can tomato sauce
1 (2-inch) stick cinnamon
¼ teaspoon salt
⅛ teaspoon pepper

Make 12 small slits on outside of roast; stuff with garlic and cloves. Brown roast on all sides in butter in a Dutch oven.

Add remaining ingredients; cover and simmer 2 hours and 15 minutes or until roast is tender. Transfer roast to serving platter. Remove cinnamon; serve pan drippings with roast. Yield: 14 to 16 servings.

## VEAL POT ROAST WITH DUMPLINGS

1 (2- to 3-pound) veal rump
  roast
2 tablespoons shortening
½ teaspoon salt
¼ teaspoon pepper
1 cup water
2 cups all-purpose flour
1 tablespoon plus 1 teaspoon
  baking powder
½ teaspoon salt
2 teaspoons lard
¾ cup milk

Brown roast on all sides in shortening in a large Dutch oven; sprinkle with salt and pepper. Add water; bring to a boil. Reduce heat; cover and simmer over low heat 1 hour and 40 minutes or until tender. Transfer roast to a serving platter. Reserve pan drippings.

Sift together flour, baking powder, and salt; cut in lard with a pastry blender until mixture resembles coarse meal. Add milk, stirring just until dry ingredients are moistened.

Bring pan drippings to a boil. Drop batter by heaping teaspoonfuls into pan drippings. Reduce heat; cover and cook over low heat 15 minutes. Serve gravy and dumplings with veal roast. Yield: 8 servings.

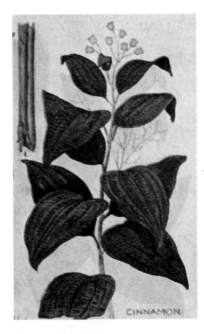

CINNAMON

## DAUBE GLACÉ

1 (3- to 4-pound) veal
  rump roast
1 tablespoon shortening,
  melted
3 medium onions,
  chopped
3 carrots, coarsely
  chopped
1 stalk celery, chopped
1 medium-size green
  pepper, seeded and
  chopped
¼ cup chopped fresh
  parsley
1 clove garlic, minced
2 bay leaves
6 whole cloves
½ teaspoon salt
½ teaspoon ground
  allspice
¼ teaspoon dried whole
  thyme
¼ teaspoon pepper
⅛ teaspoon red pepper
2 lemons, sliced
Cheesecloth
2 egg whites, unbeaten
4 envelopes unflavored
  gelatin
1 cup cold water
Fresh parsley sprigs (optional)

Brown roast on all sides in shortening in a Dutch oven. Cover roast with water. Combine next 13 ingredients (vegetables and spices); pour over roast. Cover and simmer 2 hours or until meat is tender. Remove roast; cool 10 minutes. Slice and arrange attractively on a deep serving platter; garnish with lemon slices. Set aside.

Line large strainer with cheesecloth; strain pan liquid, reserving 2 cups liquid. Discard vegetables and spices. Pour reserved liquid into a medium saucepan; add egg whites. Simmer (do not boil) 10 minutes. Line strainer with cheesecloth; strain liquid, and discard egg whites.

Soften gelatin in cold water 5 minutes; add reserved hot liquid, stirring until gelatin is dissolved. Pour gelatin mixture over sliced roast and lemon slices; chill until firm. Garnish with fresh parsley, if desired. Yield: 10 to 12 servings.

# BREADED AND SAUCED

## BAKED VEAL CHOPS

4 (1-inch-thick) veal loin
   chops
1 teaspoon salt
½ cup all-purpose flour
2 eggs, beaten
½ cup fine dry breadcrumbs
¼ cup bacon drippings
¼ cup hot water

Sprinkle chops with salt; dredge in flour. Dip chops in egg; dredge in breadcrumbs.

Brown chops in bacon drippings in a large skillet over medium heat. Transfer chops to a 12- x 8- x 2-inch baking dish. Pour hot water around chops. Bake at 350° for 45 minutes or until chops are tender. Yield: 4 servings.

*Breaded Veal Chops are served, for a pleasant change, on top of Tomato Sauce instead of under it and garnished with lemon.*

## BREADED VEAL CHOPS

4 (¾-inch-thick) veal loin
   chops
½ teaspoon salt
⅛ teaspoon white pepper
1 egg, beaten
1 teaspoon water
1 cup fine dry breadcrumbs
½ cup vegetable oil
Lemon slices (optional)

Sprinkle chops on both sides with salt and pepper. Combine egg and water. Dip chops in egg mixture, and dredge in breadcrumbs, coating well.

Heat oil in a heavy skillet over medium heat. Add chops, and cook 5 minutes on each side or until golden brown. Garnish with lemon slices, if desired. Yield: 4 servings.

*Serving Suggestion*: Serve with Tomato Sauce, page 128, if desired.

**P**roof that nothing is newer than the old is this 1847 recipe for Journey Veal from *The Carolina Housewife*. It would be delicious served as a pâté or as a picnic dish: "Cut a hard boiled egg in thin slices, and place in the middle of a bowl. Put then a layer of raw veal cut in thin slices, and sprinkled with a mixture of pepper, salt, and herbs. . . . Place next very thin slices of bacon; and continue alternating layers . . . till the bowl is full. Mash it down and tie a floured towel tight over it, turn it down in a pot of hot water, and let it boil two hours. It is eaten cold."

## VEAL CHOPS IN CREAM SAUCE

6 (¾-inch-thick) veal loin chops
½ teaspoon salt
¼ teaspoon pepper
2 eggs, beaten
1 tablespoon water
½ cup all-purpose flour
¼ cup plus 2 tablespoons vegetable oil
2 tablespoons chopped onion
2 cups sliced fresh mushrooms
1 tablespoon all-purpose flour
1 cup half-and-half, divided
2 tablespoons cognac
2 egg yolks
½ cup slivered almonds
¼ cup butter or margarine
Hot cooked noodles (optional)

Sprinkle chops with salt and pepper. Combine egg and water. Dip chops in egg mixture, and dredge in flour, coating well.

Heat oil in a large, heavy skillet over medium heat. Add chops and cook 5 minutes on each side or until golden brown. Cover and cook an additional 5 minutes. Remove chops to a warm serving platter, reserving drippings in skillet.

Sauté onion in drippings until tender. Add mushrooms; cover and cook 5 minutes.

Add 1 tablespoon flour to onion-mushroom mixture, stirring until smooth. Gradually add ½ cup half-and-half; cook over medium heat, stirring constantly, until mixture comes to a boil. Remove skillet from heat; stir in cognac.

Beat egg yolks and stir into remaining ½ cup half-and-half. Return skillet to medium heat; gradually add egg yolk mixture to hot sauce, stirring constantly, until thickened and bubbly. Remove from heat.

Sauté almonds in ¼ cup butter in a small saucepan over low heat just until almonds are lightly browned.

Pour sauce over veal chops; serve over noodles, if desired. Sprinkle with almonds. Yield: 6 servings.

## VEAL LOIN CHOPS WITH ASPARAGUS

6 (1-inch-thick) veal loin chops
¼ cup all-purpose flour
¼ cup butter or margarine, divided
½ cup dry white wine
½ teaspoon dried whole basil
¼ teaspoon salt
⅛ teaspoon pepper
1 cup chicken broth
1 (8-ounce) carton commercial sour cream
¼ teaspoon paprika
2 (10-ounce) packages frozen asparagus, cooked according to package directions

Dredge chops in flour; reserve remaining flour. Melt 3 tablespoons butter in a large, heavy skillet; brown chops on both sides. Add next 4 ingredients. Cover and simmer 30 minutes or until chops are tender. Remove chops to a warm serving platter; reserve pan drippings.

Add remaining butter to pan drippings; add reserved flour, stirring until smooth. Cook 1 minute, stirring constantly.

Gradually add chicken broth, sour cream, and paprika; mix well. Cook over medium heat, stirring constantly, until thickened and bubbly.

Arrange asparagus around chops on serving platter; serve with sour cream sauce. Yield: 6 servings.

## VEAL CHOPS IN CASSEROLE

¼ cup all-purpose flour
½ teaspoon salt
¼ teaspoon pepper
⅛ teaspoon paprika
4 (1-inch-thick) veal loin chops
3 tablespoons bacon drippings
1 tablespoon butter or margarine
1 tablespoon all-purpose flour
1 cup beef broth
2 tablespoons catsup
2 teaspoons Worcestershire sauce
2 tablespoons minced pimiento-stuffed olives
1 clove garlic, minced

Combine first 4 ingredients; dredge chops in flour mixture. Brown on both sides in hot bacon drippings. Drain chops well, and place in a 2½-quart shallow baking dish. Reserve 2 tablespoons pan drippings in skillet; add butter and 1 tablespoon flour, stirring until smooth. Cook until mixture browns, stirring constantly.

Combine remaining ingredients; gradually add to flour mixture. Cook over medium heat, stirring constantly, until thickened and bubbly. Pour over chops; cover and bake at 375° for 1 hour or until chops are tender. Remove chops to serving platter; spoon sauce over chops. Yield: 4 servings.

*Nineteenth-century housewives in close communion with dressy butchers.*

## VEAL LORRAINE

4 slices bacon, diced
1 tablespoon butter or
  margarine
8 (½-inch-thick) boneless veal
  rib chops
¼ teaspoon salt
⅛ teaspoon pepper
½ cup sliced fresh
  mushrooms
2 green onions, chopped
1 tablespoon chopped fresh
  parsley
½ cup beef broth
½ cup dry white wine
2 egg yolks, beaten
1 teaspoon lemon juice

Sauté bacon in butter in a large heavy skillet. Add chops; sprinkle chops with salt and pepper. Cook over low heat 10 minutes, turning to brown both sides. Remove bacon and chops, using a slotted spoon. Reserve pan drippings in skillet. Add mushrooms, green onion, and parsley to pan drippings; cook 1 to 2 minutes. Stir in beef broth and wine. Cook 5 minutes over low heat.

Remove from heat. Gradually stir about one-fourth of hot mixture into yolks; add to remaining hot mixture, stirring constantly. Return to low heat; cook, stirring constantly, until thickened and smooth. Return chops and bacon to sauce; stir in lemon juice. Remove chops to a serving platter. Spoon gravy over chops to serve. Yield: 8 servings.

Many cultures are represented in the South's numerous veal recipes. Not surprisingly, immigrants from many countries knew and even preferred veal to beef, because they knew from experience that if a beef animal survived a harsh winter, the meat would be tough. As we can see, from Veal Lorraine through Wiener schnitzel to the Italian scallopini and Parmigiana, Europeans who came here to be Southerners were unanimously pro-veal.

# VEAL CHOPS WITH MUSHROOMS

4 (½-inch-thick) veal loin chops
2 tablespoons butter or margarine
1 tablespoon all-purpose flour
1 (4½-ounce) jar whole mushrooms, undrained
½ cup beef broth
¼ teaspoon salt
¼ teaspoon pepper
Fresh parsley sprigs

Place chops on broiler rack 5 to 6 inches from heating element; broil about 8 minutes on each side.

Melt butter in a heavy saucepan over low heat; add flour, stirring until smooth. Cook 1 minute, stirring constantly. Drain mushrooms, reserving liquid. Gradually add mushroom liquid and beef broth to flour mixture; cook over medium heat, stirring constantly, until thickened and bubbly. Stir in salt and pepper.

Slice mushrooms in half, and add to sauce. Cook over low heat 10 minutes. Serve sauce over chops. Garnish with parsley. Yield: 4 servings.

# GRILLADES PANÉE

2 eggs, beaten
¼ cup milk
1 teaspoon salt
½ teaspoon pepper
6 (¼-inch-thick) veal cutlets
2 cups cracker crumbs
Vegetable oil

Combine eggs, milk, salt, and pepper; mix well. Dredge cutlets in cracker crumbs; dip in egg mixture, and dredge again in cracker crumbs.

Deep fry in hot oil (375°) until golden brown. Drain on paper towels, and serve immediately. Yield: 6 servings.

*Fanciful crest hovers over smoking range as wife prepares sizzling chops to surprise her husband.*

# GRILLADES LOUISIANE

2 (½-inch-thick) veal cutlets
1 tablespoon vegetable oil
2 tablespoons all-purpose flour
2 cups water
2 medium-size green peppers, chopped
1 large onion, chopped
2 tablespoons tomato paste
1 tablespoon chopped fresh parsley
1 teaspoon salt
½ teaspoon pepper
¼ teaspoon dried whole thyme
⅛ to ¼ teaspoon red pepper
1 bay leaf
Hot cooked rice

Brown cutlets on both sides in hot vegetable oil in a large skillet. Remove cutlets from skillet, reserving pan drippings. Cut veal cutlets in half. Set cutlets aside.

Stir 2 tablespoons flour into pan drippings. Cook, stirring constantly, 5 minutes or until flour is browned. Add remaining ingredients, except rice. Cook mixture 1 to 2 minutes. Add reserved cutlets; simmer, uncovered, 30 minutes or until cutlets are tender. Remove bay leaf, and discard. Serve cutlets with sauce over hot cooked rice. Yield: 4 servings.

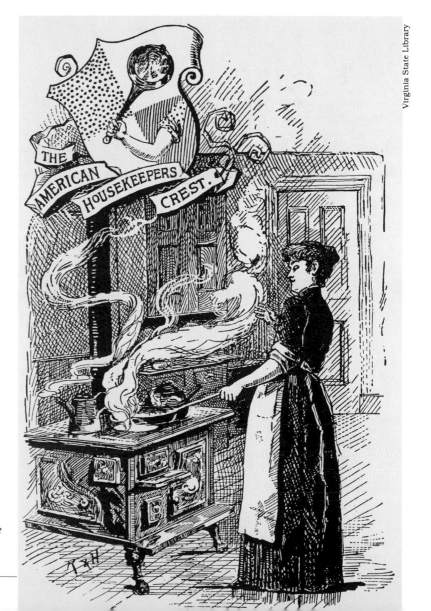

## VEAL MARSALA

1½ pounds (¼-inch-thick) veal cutlets
½ cup all-purpose flour
2 cloves garlic, minced
½ cup butter or margarine
¼ cup Marsala wine
¼ cup water
2 tablespoons Worcestershire sauce
½ teaspoon salt
⅛ teaspoon pepper
Fresh parsley sprigs (optional)
Lemon slices (optional)

Flatten veal to ⅛-inch thickness, using a meat mallet or rolling pin; dredge cutlets in flour, and set aside.

Sauté garlic in butter in a large skillet over low heat 5 minutes. Add veal; cook over medium heat 2 minutes on each side or until lightly browned. Remove veal from skillet; set aside. Reserve pan drippings.

Add wine, water, Worcestershire sauce, salt, and pepper to pan drippings, stirring well. Arrange veal over sauce mixture. Cover and simmer 30 minutes, turning veal frequently. To serve, remove cutlets to a serving platter; spoon sauce over cutlets, and garnish with parsley sprigs and lemon slices, if desired. Yield: 8 servings.

Veal Parmigiana, a true Italian dish, takes its name from Parmesan cheese, which originated in Parma in North Central Italy.

## PAPRIKA VEAL

4 (½-inch-thick) veal cutlets
1 teaspoon salt
½ teaspoon pepper
⅔ cup all-purpose flour
1 teaspoon paprika
¼ cup plus 2 tablespoons vegetable oil
1 large onion, sliced and separated into rings
¾ cup water
½ cup commercial sour cream
Fresh parsley sprigs

Sprinkle cutlets with salt and pepper. Dredge in flour, coating well. Sprinkle with paprika.

Sauté cutlets in oil in a large skillet over medium heat 5 minutes on each side or until lightly browned. Remove cutlets from skillet to a paper towel, and discard pan drippings.

Return cutlets to skillet, and top with onion rings. Add water; cover and cook over low heat 45 minutes or until onion is tender. Remove from heat. Stir in sour cream just before serving. Transfer cutlets to a serving platter. Spoon sauce over top and garnish with parsley. Yield: 4 servings.

## VEAL PARMIGIANA

¼ cup grated Parmesan cheese
2 eggs, beaten
½ teaspoon salt
⅛ teaspoon pepper
8 (⅛-inch-thick) veal cutlets
1 cup fine dry breadcrumbs
¼ cup plus 2 tablespoons olive oil
2 (8-ounce) cans tomato sauce
1 (8-ounce) package sliced mozzarella cheese

Combine Parmesan cheese, eggs, salt, and pepper; beat well. Dip cutlets into egg mixture; dredge in breadcrumbs. Sauté cutlets in oil in a skillet over medium heat 4 minutes on each side or until browned.

Place cutlets in a well-greased 2-quart casserole. Pour tomato sauce over veal; top with mozzarella cheese. Bake at 350° for 15 minutes or until cheese melts. Yield: 4 to 6 servings.

## HOTEL ROANOKE VEAL PICCATA

16 (1-ounce) veal cutlets
1 large cucumber, peeled and cut into ¼-inch-thick slices
1½ teaspoons salt
¾ teaspoon pepper
½ cup all-purpose flour
2 tablespoons vegetable oil
1 cup Chablis or other dry white wine
¼ cup chopped fresh parsley
2 tablespoons lemon juice
1 tablespoon capers
½ cup butter or margarine, melted

Sprinkle cutlets and cucumber slices with salt and pepper. Dredge in flour. Sauté veal and cucumber in oil until browned on both sides; remove from skillet. Discard pan drippings.

Stir wine, parsley, lemon juice and capers into skillet; cook over low heat 1 to 2 minutes. Stir in butter; simmer 5 minutes. Place veal and cucumbers in skillet; bring to a boil. Remove from heat. Arrange cutlets and cucumber slices on a serving platter; spoon sauce over top. Yield: 4 to 6 servings.

Since 1882, when the Norfolk and Western Railway completed the Hotel Roanoke, guests have lived for just one thing: a return visit to the queen of the Blue Ridge Mountains in Virginia. Her welcome includes the hospitable lobby filled with antiques and flowers and an impeccable dining room that spoils one for ordinary living.

*The Regency Room at the Hotel Roanoke, renowned for fine dining since 1882.*

Courtesy of the Hotel Roanoke

H annah Glasse in *The Art of Cookery* called them collops, those tender bits of veal we know as scallops. The French term is *escalopes*, and in Italy they do delicious tricks with scallopini. By any name, scallops of veal are a delicacy people of many nationalities eat as often as they can afford them.

Photographer: M.E. Warren

*Steaming crabs in such quantity is a man-sized job.*

## VEAL SCALLOPINI MARYLAND

8 (¼-inch-thick) veal cutlets
½ cup all-purpose flour
½ teaspoon salt
⅛ teaspoon pepper
¼ cup clarified butter
¼ cup butter or margarine
1½ tablespoons lemon juice
1 tablespoon dry white wine
1 tablespoon chopped fresh parsley
½ teaspoon Dijon mustard
¼ teaspoon Worcestershire sauce
1 cup fresh crabmeat, drained and flaked
2 ounces prosciutto ham, cut into ⅛-inch strips

Flatten veal to ⅛-inch thickness, using a meat mallet or rolling pin. Combine flour, salt, and pepper; mix well. Dredge veal in flour mixture.

Heat clarified butter in a large skillet over medium heat; add veal, and cook 2 minutes on each side or until lightly browned. Remove from pan, and keep warm.

Place ¼ cup butter, lemon juice, wine, parsley, mustard, and Worcestershire sauce in a small saucepan. Bring to a boil; reduce heat, and simmer 5 minutes. Add crabmeat and ham, tossing until thoroughly mixed. Spoon mixture over cutlets to serve. Yield: 8 servings.

*Veal Scallopini Maryland*

## VEAL CUTLETS PROVENÇAL

⅓ cup all-purpose flour
½ teaspoon salt
¼ teaspoon pepper
6 (¼-inch-thick) veal cutlets
¼ cup olive oil
¼ pound fresh mushrooms, sliced
1 clove garlic, minced
2 medium tomatoes, peeled and chopped
¼ cup Chablis or other dry white wine
**Dash of hot sauce**
**Minced fresh parsley**

Combine flour, salt, and pepper; mix well. Dredge cutlets in flour mixture, and brown in oil in a large skillet. Add mushrooms and garlic; cook over medium heat 5 minutes or until mushrooms are tender.

Add tomatoes, wine, and hot sauce, stirring gently. Cover and simmer 45 minutes or until cutlets are tender. Transfer cutlets to a warm serving platter; spoon sauce over cutlets, and sprinkle with minced fresh parsley. Serve immediately. Yield: 6 servings.

## VEAL SCALLOPINI

8 (¼-inch-thick) veal cutlets
¼ cup vegetable oil
¾ cup chopped onion
¼ pound fresh mushrooms, sliced
1 clove garlic, minced
2 tablespoons all-purpose flour
1 teaspoon salt
¼ teaspoon pepper
½ cup Chablis or other dry white wine
¼ cup water

Sauté cutlets in oil 4 minutes or until browned. Drain on paper towels; reserve drippings.

Sauté onion, mushrooms, and garlic in reserved pan drippings. Combine flour, salt, and pepper; add to sautéed vegetables, stirring well. Cook 1 minute, stirring constantly. Gradually add wine and water; cook over medium heat, stirring constantly, until thickened and bubbly. Add cutlets; cover and simmer 30 minutes or until meat is tender. Transfer cutlets to a warm serving platter; spoon sauce over top, and serve immediately. Yield: 8 servings.

# BAKED SESAME VEAL CUTLETS

1 egg, well beaten
1 (8-ounce) carton
  commercial sour cream
1½ cups all-purpose flour
1½ teaspoons baking
  powder
1 tablespoon salt
1 tablespoon paprika
½ teaspoon pepper
1 tablespoon sesame seeds
½ cup finely chopped pecans
6 (½-inch-thick) veal cutlets
1 cup butter or margarine,
  melted and divided

Combine egg and sour cream; mix well. Combine flour, baking powder, salt, paprika, pepper, sesame seeds, and pecans. Dip cutlets in sour cream mixture, and dredge in flour mixture, coating well.

Pour ½ cup melted butter in a 13- x 9- x 2-inch baking dish; arrange three cutlets in dish. Repeat procedure with remaining butter and cutlets. Bake, uncovered, at 375° for 30 minutes. Turn cutlets, and continue baking an additional 30 minutes. Cut cutlets in half to serve. Yield: 10 to 12 servings.

---

Thomas Jefferson enjoyed veal cutlets baked in paper, *en papillote*, the French way. Each cutlet was flattened and placed on a sheet of paper that had been well buttered and sprinkled with crumbs, mushrooms, and finely chopped herbs. After seasoning with salt and pepper, the cutlet was covered with another sheet of buttered paper, and the two papers were crimped tightly all around the edge. Tied with thread, the packages were placed on a baking pan and baked for an hour in a moderate oven.

# WIENER SCHNITZEL

6 (¼-inch-thick) veal cutlets
1 cup all-purpose flour
1 teaspoon dried parsley
  flakes
1 teaspoon salt
½ teaspoon pepper
¼ teaspoon paprika
¼ teaspoon ground cloves
1 egg, beaten
1 cup milk
½ cup butter or margarine,
  divided
2½ tablespoons lemon juice

Flatten cutlets to ⅛-inch thickness, using a meat mallet or rolling pin. Set aside.

Combine flour, parsley flakes, salt, pepper, paprika, and cloves, mixing well. Combine egg and milk; beat well. Dredge cutlets in flour mixture; dip in milk mixture, and dredge again in flour mixture.

Sauté cutlets in ¼ cup butter in a large skillet over medium heat 3 minutes on each side or until browned. Add more butter, if needed. Place cutlets on a serving platter; keep warm.

Combine remaining ¼ cup butter and lemon juice in a small saucepan. Cook over low heat just until butter melts. Pour sauce over cutlets to serve. Yield: 4 to 6 servings.

# VEAL BIRDS

½ pound bulk pork sausage
1 medium onion, chopped
2 cups herb-seasoned
  stuffing mix
¼ cup chopped fresh
  celery leaves
¼ cup chopped fresh
  parsley
1 cup plus 2 tablespoons
  water, divided
1 teaspoon salt
¼ teaspoon pepper
8 (¼-pound) veal cutlets
½ cup all-purpose flour
3 tablespoons butter or
  margarine, melted
1 medium onion, sliced
½ pound fresh mushrooms,
  sliced
Fresh celery leaves (optional)

Combine sausage and chopped onion in a medium skillet; cook over medium heat until browned, stirring to crumble meat. Drain. Combine sausage mixture, stuffing mix, chopped celery leaves, parsley, 2 tablespoons water, salt, and pepper; mix well. Set aside.

Flatten cutlets to ⅛-inch thickness, using a meat mallet or a rolling pin; place ¼ cup stuffing mixture on each veal cutlet. Fold cutlet over stuffing mixture, and secure with wooden picks.

Dredge each veal bird in flour, and brown in butter in a large skillet. Add remaining water, sliced onion, and mushrooms; cover and simmer 45 minutes or until veal is tender. Transfer veal birds, onions, and mushrooms to a warm serving platter; garnish with celery leaves, if desired. Yield: 8 servings.

*An appropriately designed check for livestock merchants.*

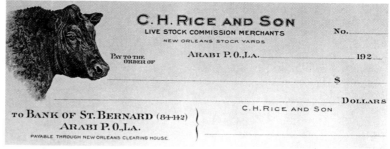

*German immigrants in the garden of their new home in Texas.*

## VEAL BIRDS WITH SOUR CREAM

1¼ cups soft breadcrumbs
½ cup chopped celery
2 teaspoons finely chopped onion
½ teaspoon salt
¼ teaspoon pepper
⅛ teaspoon rubbed sage
¼ cup plus 1 tablespoon butter or margarine, melted and divided
1 pound veal steak, cut ¼-inch thick
½ cup all-purpose flour
1 (10¾-ounce) can chicken broth
1 teaspoon all-purpose flour
1 (8-ounce) carton commercial sour cream

Combine breadcrumbs, celery, onion, salt, pepper, sage, and 3 tablespoons melted butter; mix well, and set aside.

Place steak between two sheets of waxed paper. Flatten to ⅛-inch thickness, using a meat mallet or a rolling pin. Cut steak into 8 portions. Place 2 tablespoons stuffing down the center of each piece. Roll up jellyroll fashion, and tie securely with string.

Dredge each veal bird in ½ cup flour. Brown in remaining melted butter in a heavy skillet over medium heat. Add chicken broth; cover and simmer 30 minutes or until veal is tender. Transfer veal birds to a warm serving platter, reserving pan drippings.

Combine 1 teaspoon flour and sour cream, stirring until well blended. Add sour cream mixture to pan drippings. Cook over low heat 10 minutes or until thickened, stirring constantly. Spoon sauce over veal birds to serve. Yield: 4 to 6 servings.

*The best-selling cookbook by Hannah Glasse was first published in 1747, and for many years was thought to have been written by a man.*

# THE
# ART
OF
# COOKERY,

Made PLAIN and EASY;

Which far exceeds any THING of the Kind ever yet Publifhed.

CONTAINING,

I. Of Roafting, Boiling, &c.
II. Of Made-Difhes.
III. Read this Chapter, and you will find how Expenfive a French Cook's Sauce is.
IV. To make a Number of pretty little Difhes fit for a Supper, or Side Difh, and little Corner-Difhes for a great Table; and the reft you have in the Chapter for Lent.
V. To drefs Fifh.
VI. Of Soops and Broths.
VII. Of Puddings.
VIII. Of Pies.
IX. For a Faft-Dinner, a Number of good Difhes, which you may make ufe for a Table at any other Time.
X. Directions for the Sick.
XI. For Captains of Ships.
XII. Of Hog's Puddings, Saufages, &c.

XIII. To Pot and Make Hams, &c.
XIV. Of Pickling.
XV. Of Making Cakes, &c.
XVI. Of Cheefecakes, Creams, Jellies, Whip Syllabubs, &c.
XVII. Of Made Wines, Brewing, French Bread, Muffins, &c.
XVIII. Jarring Cherries, and Preferves, &c.
XIX. To Make Anchovies, Vermicella, Ketchup, Vinegar, and to keep Artichokes, French-Beans, &c.
XX. Of Diftilling.
XXI. How to Market, and the Seafons of the Year for Butcher's Meat, Poultry, Fifh, Herbs, Roots, &c. and Fruit.
XXII. A certain Cure for the Bite of a Mad Dog. By Dr. Mead.

BY A LADY.

## HANNAH GLASSE'S VEAL COLLOPS WITH OYSTER FORCEMEAT

8 (¼-inch-thick) veal cutlets
8 fresh oysters
3 slices bacon
1 tablespoon chopped fresh parsley
½ teaspoon salt
¼ teaspoon pepper
Dash of ground nutmeg
Dash of ground mace
Dash of ground cloves
Pinch of dried whole thyme
2 tablespoons butter or margarine
½ cup beef broth
½ cup dry white wine
2 shallots, finely chopped
1 clove garlic, minced
½ pound fresh mushrooms, sliced
1 anchovy, mashed (optional)
2 tablespoons all-purpose flour
1 tablespoon butter or margarine, melted

Grind together 2 veal cutlets, oysters, and bacon in a food grinder. Add parsley, salt, pepper, nutmeg, mace, cloves, and thyme, mixing well.

Spread one-sixth ground mixture on each remaining veal cutlet. Roll up each cutlet jellyroll fashion, and secure with wooden picks.

Melt 2 tablespoons butter in a large skillet over medium heat; brown veal rolls on all sides. Transfer veal to a 2½-quart shallow baking dish, reserving pan drippings in skillet.

Add beef broth, wine, shallots, garlic, mushrooms, and anchovy, if desired, to skillet; stir well. Pour mushroom mixture over veal rolls. Cover and bake at 350° for 1 hour. Remove veal rolls to a serving platter; keep warm.

Combine flour and 1 tablespoon melted butter; add to mushroom mixture, stirring until thickened. Serve sauce over veal rolls. Yield: 6 servings.

Hannah Allgood Glasse wrote *The Art of Cookery Made Plain and Easy* in her spare time, while caring for a husband and eight children. The book was a runaway best-seller. Colonists brought it to America, and an American edition was printed in the early 1800s. Anyone curious about Hannah the person will find fact mingled with fiction. Depending on the source, she was wellborn or illegitimate. At 16, she married (a) solicitor Peter Glasse or (b) adventurer John Glasse. She died an obscure seamstress. Ah well, her fame was "undeserved," says Esther Aresty in *The Delectable Past.*

# CUBED AND GROUND

## BAKED VEAL WITH NOODLES

2 pounds veal cutlets, cut into 1-inch cubes
2 tablespoons butter or margarine
3 tablespoons water
2 tablespoons all-purpose flour
½ teaspoon salt
⅛ teaspoon paprika
1 (8-ounce) carton commercial sour cream
½ cup chopped fresh mushrooms
1 tablespoon onion juice
Hot cooked noodles

Brown veal in butter in a skillet. Transfer veal to a 2-quart casserole; reserve drippings.

Combine water and drippings in top of a double boiler; mix well. Add flour, salt, and paprika; mix until smooth. Cook 1 minute, stirring constantly, until thickened and bubbly.

Remove from heat; gradually add sour cream, mushrooms, and onion juice, mixing well. Pour over veal; cover and bake at 300° for 1 hour. Serve over noodles. Yield: 6 to 8 servings.

## VEAL CURRY

¼ cup butter or margarine
1½ pounds veal cutlets, cut into 4-inch strips
1 medium onion, chopped
1½ to 2 teaspoons curry powder
1½ cups half-and-half
¼ cup water
3 tablespoons all-purpose flour
1 tablespoon vinegar
½ teaspoon salt
¼ teaspoon dry mustard
⅛ teaspoon garlic powder
Hot cooked rice
Condiments

Melt butter in a large skillet; add veal, and cook until browned. Add onion; sauté until tender.

Add curry powder and half-and-half; stir well. Cover and simmer 15 minutes.

Combine water, flour, and vinegar; stir until smooth. Add flour mixture to curry mixture; cook, stirring constantly, until mixture is thickened and bubbly. Stir in salt, mustard, and garlic powder.

Serve veal mixture over hot cooked rice with several of the following condiments: (about ¾ cup each) chutney, flaked coconut, chopped hard-cooked egg, crumbled cooked bacon, salted peanuts, and sautéed onion. Yield: 4 servings.

*Baked Veal with Noodles, an easy dish on which to build a menu: Crisp salad, steamed vegetable, fresh fruit and cheese for dessert.*

## VEAL OYSTERS

1 pound boneless veal
  cutlets, cut into 1-inch
  cubes
1 egg, beaten
1 cup finely crushed saltine
  cracker crumbs
3 tablespoons vegetable oil
1 tablespoon butter or
  margarine
1 tablespoon all-purpose flour
1 cup milk
½ teaspoon salt
¼ teaspoon white pepper

Dip veal pieces in egg; dredge
in cracker crumbs. Sauté in oil
in a large skillet over medium
heat until browned. Drain veal
on paper towels; set aside.

Melt butter in a heavy saucepan over low heat. Add flour;
stir until smooth. Cook 1 minute, stirring constantly. Gradually add milk; cook over medium
heat, stirring constantly, until
thickened and bubbly. Stir in
salt and pepper.

Place veal in a lightly greased
1-quart casserole. Spoon sauce
over veal. Bake, uncovered, at
325° for 1 hour or until veal is
tender. Yield: 2 to 4 servings.

## VEAL AND NOODLE STEW

2 pounds veal stew meat, cut
  into 1-inch cubes
1 large onion, chopped
2 tablespoons vegetable oil
⅔ cup water
1 (5-ounce) package egg
  noodles, cooked and
  drained
½ cup chopped fresh
  mushrooms
1 teaspoon salt
½ teaspoon white pepper
1 (8-ounce) carton
  commercial sour cream

Sauté veal and onion in oil in
a large skillet until veal is no
longer pink. Add water; cover
and simmer 1 hour. Stir in noodles, mushrooms, salt, pepper,
and sour cream. Spoon into a
lightly greased 2-quart casserole. Bake at 300° for 45 minutes. Yield: 6 to 8 servings.

*Annie Dennis*

## VEAL FRICASSEE

1 pound boneless veal
  cutlets, cut into 1-inch
  cubes
⅓ cup butter or margarine,
  melted
1½ cups water
3 new potatoes, peeled and
  thinly sliced
2 small onions, thinly sliced
2 teaspoons salt
½ teaspoon coarsely ground
  black pepper
1 clove garlic, minced
2 tablespoons chopped fresh
  parsley
2 tablespoons all-purpose
  flour
1 cup milk

Cook veal in butter in a small
Dutch oven over medium heat,
turning once to brown both
sides. Add water, potatoes,
onion, salt, pepper, garlic, and
parsley. Cover and cook over low
heat 1 hour and 10 minutes or
until veal is tender.

Combine flour and milk, mixing well. Gradually stir flour
mixture into veal mixture; cook
over medium heat 5 minutes or
until mixture is thickened and
bubbly. Yield: 4 servings.

A nnie Dennis's recipe
for "Veal Oysters,"
from her 1901 cook-
book: "Select nice white veal,
cut in pieces the size of an
oyster, pound well, dip in
beaten egg, roll in cracker
dust, and fry in boiling lard
as oysters. A delicious man-
nor [*sic*] of cooking veal."

## VEAL IN PAPRIKA CREAM

3 to 4 pounds veal stew meat,
  cut into 1-inch cubes
1 clove garlic, minced
½ cup butter or margarine
¼ cup plus 2 tablespoons
  all-purpose flour
2 (10½-ounce) cans beef
  consommé
1 tablespoon lemon juice
1 tablespoon paprika
1 bay leaf
1 pound small boiling onions,
  peeled
1 cup dry white wine
½ cup commercial sour
  cream
Hot cooked noodles

Sauté veal and garlic in butter
in a large Dutch oven until veal
is no longer pink. Stir in flour.
Add consommé, lemon juice, paprika, and bay leaf. Simmer, uncovered, 1 hour over low heat.

Place onions and water to
cover in a saucepan. Bring to a
boil; reduce heat. Cover; simmer 10 minutes. Drain.

Add onions and wine to veal
mixture. Simmer, uncovered,
20 minutes or until onions are
tender. Remove from heat; discard bay leaf, and stir in sour
cream. Serve over hot cooked
noodles. Yield: 8 servings.

## VEAL STEW

4 slices slab bacon
1 (2- to 3-pound) rump of veal, cut into 1-inch cubes
1 teaspoon salt
½ teaspoon pepper
2 cups water
1 cup cubed carrots
1 (14½-ounce) can whole tomatoes, undrained
1 (17-ounce) can whole kernel corn, drained
6 small onions, halved
1 tablespoon chopped fresh parsley
1 teaspoon Worcestershire sauce
4 medium potatoes, peeled and quartered

Cook bacon in a large Dutch oven until crisp; remove bacon, and crumble. Reserve bacon drippings in Dutch oven.

Sprinkle veal with salt and pepper; sauté veal in drippings until browned. Add bacon, water, carrots, tomatoes, corn, onions, parsley, and Worcestershire sauce; cover and simmer 1 hour. Add potatoes; cover and simmer about 30 minutes. Yield: 8 to 10 servings.

## VEAL LOAF

1½ pounds ground veal
½ pound ground pork
1 cup soft breadcrumbs
2 eggs
2 tablespoons minced onion
2 tablespoons chopped fresh parsley
½ teaspoon garlic powder
¼ teaspoon salt
⅛ teaspoon pepper
1 cup water
Cherry tomatoes (optional)
Fresh parsley sprigs (optional)

Combine veal, pork, breadcrumbs, eggs, onion, chopped parsley, garlic powder, salt, and pepper; mix well. Shape meat mixture into a loaf; place in a lightly greased 13- x 9- x 2-inch baking dish. Bake at 350° for 20 minutes.

Pour water over loaf, and bake an additional 40 minutes. Remove veal loaf to a warm platter; garnish with cherry tomatoes and parsley, if desired. Yield: 6 servings.

*Note*: This loaf is delicious served hot as well as when served cold on whole wheat bread with Dijon mustard.

Some late nineteenth-century cookbooks contained recipes for "Blind Hare" or "Blind Rabbit." We know it as meat loaf. Note the heavy spicing in this one dated 1877: "3 pounds of minced veal, 3 pounds of minced beef, 8 eggs, well beaten, 3 stale rolls, or the same amount of bread-crumbs, pepper, salt, 2 grated nutmegs, a heaping tablespoonful of ground cinnamon. Mix all well together. Form it into an oval shaped loaf, smooth it, and sprinkle bread or cracker crumbs over the top. Bake it in a moderate oven about 3 hours. It is to be sliced when cold."

*Practical Cooking and Dinner Giving,*
*1877, by Mary F. Henderson*

*Veal Loaf with pork added for moistness. Herbed and spiced, it's as good cold as hot, if any is left!*

*Hors d'oeuvres table with ever-popular meatballs.*

## VEAL MEATBALLS

1½ pounds ground veal
1 cup fine dry breadcrumbs
2 eggs, beaten
½ cup milk
1 clove garlic, minced
1½ teaspoons salt
¼ teaspoon pepper
3 tablespoons vegetable oil
3 tablespoons minced onion
3 tablespoons all-purpose
   flour
1 (16-ounce) carton
   commercial sour cream
1 tablespoon Worcestershire
   sauce
1 (4½-ounce) jar sliced
   mushrooms, undrained
Hot cooked noodles
1 teaspoon poppy seeds

Combine first 7 ingredients; mix well. Shape into 1½-inch balls; brown in oil in a Dutch oven over medium heat. Remove meatballs and drain; reserve drippings. Cook onion in drippings until tender. Add flour; stir constantly.

Combine sour cream and Worcestershire sauce; gradually add to onion mixture, stirring constantly, until thickened. Add mushrooms and meatballs; gently turn to coat. Cover; simmer 30 minutes over low heat. Serve over hot cooked noodles, and sprinkle with poppy seeds. Yield: 8 servings.

When did meatballs hit the cocktail party circuit? No exact date, but an 1847 recipe for Beef Balls in *The Carolina Housewife* calls for minced beef and onions, boiled parsley, grated breadcrumbs, salt, pepper, and nutmeg. The instructions are clear: "Mix the whole together; moisten with a beaten egg. Roll into balls, flour and fry them."

## VEAL CROQUETTES

1½ tablespoons shortening
3 tablespoons all-purpose
   flour
¾ cup milk
2 cups cooked ground veal
2 teaspoons chopped fresh
   parsley
1 teaspoon lemon juice
1 teaspoon onion juice
1 teaspoon salt
½ cup fine dry breadcrumbs
1 egg, beaten
Vegetable oil

Melt shortening in a heavy saucepan over low heat; add flour, and cook 1 minute, stirring constantly. Gradually add milk; cook over medium heat, stirring constantly, until thickened. Stir in veal, parsley, lemon juice, onion juice, and salt; chill 1 hour.

Shape veal into 6 croquettes; roll in breadcrumbs. Dip in egg; roll in breadcrumbs. Deep fry croquettes in hot oil (375°) until golden brown. Yield: 6 servings.

## VEAL SOUFFLÉ

¼ cup plus 2 tablespoons
  butter or margarine
½ cup all-purpose flour
3 cups milk
3 cups cooked ground veal
½ cup soft breadcrumbs
4 eggs, separated
2 tablespoons chopped fresh
  parsley
1¼ teaspoons salt
¾ teaspoon pepper

Melt butter in a medium saucepan over low heat; add flour, stirring until smooth. Cook 1 minute, stirring constantly. Gradually add milk; cook over medium heat, stirring constantly, until thickened and bubbly. Add veal, breadcrumbs, egg yolks, parsley, salt, and pepper, mixing well.

Beat egg whites (at room temperature) until stiff. Gently fold egg whites into veal mixture. Spoon into eight 6-ounce well-greased custard cups. Bake at 325° for 40 minutes or until a knife inserted in center comes out clean. Yield: 8 servings.

## WOODSTOCK

1 tablespoon butter or
  margarine
1 tablespoon all-purpose flour
1 cup milk
1 cup cooked, chopped veal
1 (4½-ounce) jar sliced
  mushrooms, drained
2 hard-cooked eggs, chopped
2 tablespoons chopped
  pimiento
½ teaspoon Worcestershire
  sauce
Dash of hot sauce
½ teaspoon salt
6 patty shells, baked

Melt butter in a saucepan over low heat; add flour, and cook 1 minute, stirring constantly. Gradually add milk; cook over medium heat, stirring constantly, until thickened.

Stir in veal, mushrooms, egg, pimiento, Worcestershire sauce, hot sauce, and salt; cook until hot. Spoon into patty shells and serve. Yield: 6 servings.

# LAMB

## Once a Gift of Spring,
## Now a Year-Round Favorite

L amb was defined in 1930 as the meat of a sheep six weeks to three months old; this is "milk" lamb. Today, scientific breeding has brought palatable "grass" lamb to our tables so that we may be eating the meat of an animal up to a year old.

Mature mutton was a staple in Eastern countries from Biblical days and, in due time, in pastoral Europe. For centuries, the English appetite for mutton was evidenced by any literary work that made reference to dining. An author had only to mention a saddle or a haunch or a boiled leg of mutton to conjure a vision of feasting.

Mutton, then, was a built-in favorite with the English colonials. Predators and chronic shortage of food for the sheep made the meat increasingly dear. Yet when important guests were entertained, every effort was made to put mutton on the table. As late as 1833, when a distinguished New Englander dined with the Barber family in Staunton, Virginia, "a boiled mutton" was part of the sumptuous repast.

Unaccountably, around 1890, mutton began to decline, while lamb rose in popularity. Farming in the South had taken on a civilized aspect. More land was cleared for grazing and, in contrast to the Western lamb growers' problem with the coyote even today, the loss to wild animals abated. People could afford to slaughter younger lambs. There is also a distinct possibility that the term lamb became more chic than mutton for the same viand.

Mutton's slide from favor is chronicled in cookbooks: In 1860, *The Virginia Housewife* contained a third as many recipes for lamb as for mutton. *The New Annie Dennis Cookbook*, 1901, gave the meats equal space. By 1924, in *The Modern Priscilla Cookbook*, the score was lamb, eleven; mutton, one. However, the western half of Kentucky does not know that mutton is passé; mutton is barbecued by the ton every year for the church and political picnics there.

*Rack of Lamb (page 84). A pair of racks with bones interlaced at top for a stunning presentation. Sauce is wine and butter.*

# THE CROWN ROAST

*Wine keg*

## RACK OF LAMB

2 tablespoons vegetable oil
¼ teaspoon salt
¼ teaspoon pepper
¼ teaspoon dried whole
   oregano
⅛ teaspoon garlic powder
2 (1½- to 2-pound) racks of
   lamb
½ cup chopped fresh parsley
1 cup Burgundy or other dry
   red wine
½ cup butter

Combine oil, salt, pepper, oregano, and garlic powder; brush on lamb. Place lamb, bone ends up, in a shallow roasting pan. Insert meat thermometer, if desired.

Bake, uncovered, at 400° until desired degree of doneness: about 35 minutes or 140° (rare); about 55 minutes or 160° (medium); about 1 hour and 10 minutes or 170° (well done).

Transfer lamb to a warm serving platter, reserving pan drippings. Sprinkle with parsley. Let lamb stand 10 minutes before slicing.

Add wine to pan drippings in roasting pan. Cook over low heat, stirring with a wooden spoon to loosen browned crumbs. Add butter; simmer 4 to 5 minutes, stirring occasionally. Serve sauce with lamb. Yield: 4 servings.

## SADDLE OF LAMB

1 (4- to 5-pound) saddle of
   lamb
1 teaspoon salt
¼ teaspoon pepper
½ cup all-purpose flour,
   divided
2½ cups boiling water,
   divided
1 beef-flavored bouillon
   cube
3 tablespoons chopped fresh
   mint leaves
2 tablespoons vinegar
¼ cup butter or margarine
Fresh mint leaves (optional)

Sprinkle lamb with salt and pepper; dredge in ¼ cup flour. Place lamb, fat side up, in a large Dutch oven. Add 1½ cups boiling water. Cover and bake at 350° for 1½ hours or until lamb is tender, basting occasionally with pan liquid. Transfer lamb to a warm serving platter, reserving pan liquid; keep warm.

Dissolve bouillon cube in remaining 1 cup water in a small mixing bowl; add chopped mint, vinegar, and reserved pan liquid, mixing well. Set aside.

Melt butter in a saucepan; cook until golden brown. Add remaining ¼ cup flour, stirring until smooth. Cook over medium heat 1 minute, stirring constantly. Gradually add mint mixture. Cook over medium heat, stirring constantly, until thickened and bubbly. Strain. Serve sauce with lamb. Garnish with fresh mint leaves, if desired. Yield: 4 servings.

Of a visit to Shirley Plantation in 1833, Henry Barnard, a principal of St. John's College, Annapolis, wrote: "At dinner Mrs. Carter sat at one end of the table with a large dish of rich soup, and Mr. C. at the other, with a saddle of fine mutton. . . ." Such meals had doubtless been served at Shirley for generations by the time Barnard paid his visit. The setting of the table, according to the writer, was superintended by a servant who had been doing so for fifty years.

*Sheep on White House lawn, 1919, quietly "mowing" grass.*

## CROWN ROAST OF LAMB WITH FRUIT DRESSING

2 tablespoons olive oil
1 teaspoon salt
1 teaspoon pepper
1 (5- to 6-pound) crown roast of lamb
Glaze (recipe follows)
Fruit Dressing
Orange slices (optional)
Maraschino cherries (optional)

Combine oil, salt, and pepper; brush surface of roast with oil mixture. Place a small piece of aluminum foil on each bone end. Place roast, bone ends up, on a greased rack in a shallow roasting pan. Insert meat thermometer, if desired.

Bake, uncovered, at 325° until desired degree of doneness: about 1 hour and 15 minutes or 140° (rare); about 2 hours or 160° (medium); about 2½ hours or 170° (well done). Baste with glaze during last 30 minutes.

Transfer roast to a warm serving platter. Spoon Fruit Dressing into center of roast. Garnish with orange slices and maraschino cherries, if desired. Yield: 6 servings.

### Glaze:

½ cup orange marmalade
3 tablespoons lemon juice
1 tablespoon brown sugar
2 teaspoons prepared mustard

Combine all ingredients in a small heavy saucepan over medium heat. Bring to a boil, stirring constantly. Remove from heat. Yield: about ½ cup.

### Fruit Dressing:

1½ cups golden raisins
1 cup sherry
2 cups peeled, chopped apple
1 cup finely chopped onion
2 cloves garlic, minced
½ cup butter or margarine
3 tablespoons chopped fresh parsley
2 tablespoons lemon juice
¼ teaspoon ground mace
⅛ teaspoon ground nutmeg
⅛ teaspoon dried whole thyme
⅛ teaspoon dried whole chervil
⅛ teaspoon dried whole rosemary, crushed
2 cups toasted seasoned breadcrumbs

Combine raisins and sherry. Let stand 2 hours.

Sauté apple, onion, and garlic in butter in a medium skillet until tender. Add raisins and sherry, parsley, lemon juice, and spices; simmer 10 minutes. Stir in breadcrumbs, tossing well. Yield: about 5 cups.

*Lemon Garlic Leg of Lamb, photographed at Travellers' Rest, a restored Nashville home built in the 1800s.*

## LEMON GARLIC LEG OF LAMB

1 (7- to 7½-pound) leg of lamb
1½ tablespoons lemon juice
3 cloves garlic, sliced
½ cup all-purpose flour
1 teaspoon salt
½ teaspoon pepper
1 tablespoon paprika
Mint or red currant jelly

Remove the fell (tissue-like covering) from lamb with a sharp knife. Place lamb, fat side up, in a shallow roasting pan. Rub surface of lamb with lemon juice. Make several small slits on outside of lamb, and stuff with garlic slices.

Combine flour, salt, pepper, and paprika; mix well. Sprinkle flour mixture over lamb, coating

well. Insert meat thermometer, if desired.

Bake, uncovered, at 400° for 15 minutes; reduce heat to 325°. Continue baking until desired degree of doneness: about 1 hour and 40 minutes or 140° (rare); about 2 hours or 160° (medium); about 2½ hours or 170° (well done).

Transfer lamb to a warm serving platter. Let stand 10 minutes before slicing. Serve lamb with mint or red currant jelly. Yield: 8 servings.

## GRILLED LAMB

1 (7- to 8-pound) leg of lamb
15 cloves garlic, sliced
1 teaspoon salt
½ teaspoon pepper
½ teaspoon dried whole oregano

Remove the fell (tissue-like covering) from lamb with a sharp knife. Make small slits on outside of lamb; stuff with garlic. Rub surface of lamb with salt, pepper, and oregano. Wrap lamb in aluminum foil.

Place lamb on grill over medium coals. Insert meat thermometer, if desired. Cover grill, and open vent. Grill until desired degree of doneness: about 2 hours or 140° (rare); about 2½ hours or 160° (medium); about 3 hours or 170° (well done).

Transfer lamb to a warm serving platter. Let lamb stand 10 minutes before slicing. Yield: 8 to 10 servings.

# OVEN-BARBECUED LAMB

1 (8½- to 9-pound) leg of
   lamb
⅔ cup all-purpose flour
1 teaspoon ground ginger
1 teaspoon dry mustard
1 teaspoon salt
½ teaspoon pepper
2 tablespoons chili sauce
2 tablespoons olive oil
1 tablespoon Worcestershire
   sauce
1 tablespoon vinegar
2 medium onions, sliced
1 clove garlic, sliced
1 cup boiling water

Remove the fell (tissue-like covering) from lamb with a sharp knife. Make small slits on outside of lamb; set aside.

Combine flour, ginger, mustard, salt, and pepper; mix well. Rub surface of lamb with flour mixture, coating well. Set aside.

Combine chili sauce, olive oil, Worcestershire sauce, and vinegar, stirring until well blended; set aside.

Place lamb, fat side up, in a shallow roasting pan. Insert meat thermometer, if desired. Arrange onion slices and garlic around lamb. Baste with chili sauce mixture.

Bake, uncovered, at 400° for 25 minutes. Reduce heat to 350°, and continue baking until desired degree of doneness: about 1 hour and 15 minutes or 140° (rare); about 1 hour and 30 minutes or 160° (medium); about 2 hours or 170° (well done). Baste every 15 minutes with chili sauce mixture. During last hour of baking add boiling water to pan.

Transfer lamb to a warm serving platter, reserving pan drippings. Let lamb stand 10 minutes before slicing.

Skim fat from pan drippings; discard fat. Spoon pan drippings over lamb to serve. Yield: 12 servings.

*Jim Chicos and Gus Safos are roasting lamb for returning dove hunters. Photographed at Katy, Texas.*

# ROAST LAMB WITH ANCHOVIES

1 (3- to 3½-pound) leg of lamb
  roast
1 (2-ounce) can anchovies,
  drained and chopped
2 cloves garlic, minced
1 teaspoon salt
½ teaspoon pepper
½ cup butter
1 (10½-ounce) can beef
  consommé
2 tablespoons all-purpose
  flour
1 (5-ounce) package wide egg
  noodles, cooked
1 tablespoon butter
1 (2-ounce) jar chopped
  pimientos, drained
1 tablespoon chopped fresh
  parsley

Remove the fell (tissue-like covering) from roast with a sharp knife. Make several small slits in surface of roast. Stuff slits with anchovies. Combine garlic, salt, and pepper; rub mixture over surface of roast.

Melt ½ cup butter in a small roaster over medium heat. Add roast; brown on all sides. Insert meat thermometer, if desired. Add consommé to roaster.

Bake, uncovered, at 325° until desired degree of doneness: about 1½ hours or 140° (rare); about 2 hours or 160° (medium); about 2½ hours or 170° (well done). Baste frequently with pan drippings.

Transfer roast to a warm serving platter, reserving pan drippings in roaster. Let roast stand 10 minutes before slicing.

Combine flour and a small amount of water to form a smooth paste. Stir mixture into pan drippings; cook over medium heat, stirring constantly, until thickened and bubbly. Set gravy aside.

Combine noodles, 1 tablespoon butter, and pimientos; toss lightly. Place noodle mixture around roast on serving platter; sprinkle with parsley. Serve roast with noodles and gravy. Yield: 6 to 8 servings.

Baltimore's Mayor Latrobe knew his mutton well enough in 1891 to ". . . suggest to the epicure to obtain a saddle of mutton from a three-year-old sheep bred from the Druid Hill flock; let it hang about a week in cold weather, then have it perfectly roasted—cooked through but not overdone, using a marinade of sweet herbs." He believed in good company and champagne to go with it.

## HERBED ROAST LAMB

1 (7- to 7½-pound) leg of lamb
2 cloves garlic, minced
1 bay leaf, crushed
1 teaspoon salt
½ teaspoon pepper
½ teaspoon ground ginger
½ teaspoon marjoram leaves
½ teaspoon rubbed sage
½ teaspoon ground thyme
1 tablespoon soy sauce
1 tablespoon vegetable oil

Remove the fell (tissue-like covering) from lamb with a sharp knife. Place lamb, fat side up, in a shallow roasting pan. Make several small slits on outside of lamb; set aside.

Combine remaining ingredients; mix well. Rub mixture over surface of lamb. Insert meat thermometer, if desired.

Bake, uncovered, at 450° for 15 minutes; reduce heat to 350°. Continue baking until desired degree of doneness: about 2 hours or 140° (rare); about 2 hours and 20 minutes or 160° (medium); about 2 hours and 40 minutes or 170° (well done).

Transfer lamb to a warm serving platter. Let stand 10 minutes before slicing. Yield: 8 to 10 servings.

*An 1880s advertisement
for oil-fired cooking stoves.*

*Sheep do grass-cutting duty on the grounds of Troth's Fortune on the Choptank River in Maryland.*

## TROTH'S FORTUNE BRAISED LEG OF LAMB

1 (5- to 6-pound) leg of lamb
1 teaspoon Italian seasoning
½ teaspoon salt
¼ teaspoon pepper
½ cup butter or margarine
4 carrots, scraped and
    diagonally sliced
2 medium onions, quartered
2 cloves garlic, minced
1 cup beef broth
¼ cup Madeira or other sweet
    wine
2 tablespoons all-purpose
    flour
¼ cup cold water

Remove the fell (tissue-like covering) from lamb with a sharp knife. Rub surface of lamb with Italian seasoning, salt, and pepper; brown lamb in butter on all sides in a large stock pot. Remove lamb; set aside. Reserve pan drippings in stock pot. Add carrots, onion, and garlic to pan drippings. Cook over medium heat until onion is tender.

Place browned lamb in stock pot over vegetables. Combine beef broth and wine; pour over lamb. Cover and simmer 3 hours or until lamb is tender, basting occasionally.

Transfer lamb and vegetables to a warm serving platter, reserving pan drippings.

Skim fat from pan drippings; discard fat. Combine 2 tablespoons flour and cold water; stir until smooth. Combine flour mixture and pan drippings; cook, stirring constantly, until mixture is thickened and bubbly. Serve gravy with lamb and vegetables. Yield: 6 servings.

# LAMB ROAST À LA BÉARNAISE

1 (3- to 4-pound) boneless leg
  of lamb roast
3 slices bacon, halved
1 tablespoon butter or
  margarine, melted
½ cup fine dry breadcrumbs,
  divided
3 shallots, minced
1 teaspoon seasoned salt
¼ teaspoon salt
⅛ teaspoon pepper
1 tablespoon lemon juice
Lemon slices (optional)

Remove the fell (tissue-like covering) from roast with a sharp knife. Insert blade of sharp knife horizontally through side of roast cutting a 1½-inch wide slit through roast; remove blade. Repeat procedure 6 times, spacing slits evenly in roast. Lay half a slice of bacon on a narrow metal spatula allowing about 1 inch of bacon to extend over end of spatula. Slide spatula completely through slit in roast. Hold bacon securely, and remove spatula leaving bacon slice in roast. Repeat procedure with remaining slices of bacon. (A larding needle may be used to insert bacon in roast.)

Place roast, fat side up, in a shallow roasting pan. Brush roast with butter.

Combine ¼ cup breadcrumbs, shallots, seasoned salt, salt, and pepper; sprinkle over roast. Insert meat thermometer, if desired.

Cover lamb lightly with well-buttered brown paper. Bake at 400° until desired degree of doneness: about 1½ hours or 140° (rare); about 2½ hours or 160° (medium); about 3 hours or 170° (well done).

Remove brown paper; sprinkle with remaining ¼ cup breadcrumbs. Continue baking 10 minutes or until breadcrumbs are browned.

Transfer roast to a warm serving platter. Sprinkle with lemon juice. Let stand 10 minutes before slicing. Garnish with lemon slices, if desired. Yield: 8 to 10 servings.

# LEG OF LAMB WITH PLUM SAUCE

1 (16-ounce) can plums
2 tablespoons lemon juice
1 tablespoon soy sauce
1 teaspoon Worcestershire
  sauce
½ teaspoon basil, crushed
½ clove garlic, minced
1 (4- to 5-pound) boneless leg
  of lamb roast
¼ teaspoon salt
⅛ teaspoon pepper
Fresh parsley sprigs (optional)

Drain plums, reserving juice; pit and sieve plums. Set plums aside. Combine plum juice with lemon juice, soy sauce, Worcestershire sauce, basil, and garlic. Mix well; set aside.

Remove the fell (tissue-like covering) from roast with a sharp knife. Place roast on a rack in a shallow roasting pan; sprinkle surface of roast with salt and pepper. Insert meat thermometer, if desired.

Bake, uncovered, at 325° until desired degree of doneness: about 1½ hours or 140° (rare); about 2 hours or 160° (medium); about 2½ hours or 170° (well done). To glaze, baste with plum juice mixture frequently during cooking time. Reserve remaining plum juice mixture.

Transfer roast to a warm serving platter, reserving pan drippings. Let roast stand 10 minutes before slicing.

Combine reserved sieved plums and remaining plum juice mixture in a small saucepan. Simmer 5 minutes, stirring occasionally.

Garnish roast with parsley, if desired, and serve with plum sauce. Yield: 6 to 8 servings.

# GLAZED LEG OF LAMB

1 (4- to 5-pound) boneless
  lamb leg roast
½ teaspoon salt
¼ teaspoon pepper
½ cup boiling water
1 vegetable-flavored bouillon
  cube
Cranberry Glaze

Remove the fell (tissue-like covering) from roast with a sharp knife. Sprinkle surface of roast with salt and pepper; place roast in a shallow roasting pan. Combine water and bouillon cube; stir until bouillon cube dissolves. Pour bouillon mixture over roast; bake, uncovered, at 325° for 30 minutes.

Remove from oven; baste with Cranberry Glaze. Insert meat thermometer, if desired.

Bake, uncovered, at 325° until desired degree of doneness: about 1 hour or 140° (rare); about 1½ hours or 160° (medium); about 2 hours or 170° (well done). Baste frequently with Cranberry Glaze.

Transfer roast to a warm serving platter, reserving pan drippings. Let roast stand 10 minutes before slicing.

Skim fat from pan drippings; discard fat. Serve pan drippings with roast. Garnish as desired. Yield: 8 servings.

**Cranberry Glaze:**

2 medium oranges
1 cup whole-berry cranberry
  sauce
1 cup orange juice
½ teaspoon ground ginger
2 tablespoons grated orange
  rind

Peel oranges; discard seeds and white membrane. Chop pulp; set aside.

Combine cranberry sauce, orange juice, ginger, and orange rind in a medium saucepan; add orange pulp, mixing well. Cook over low heat until thoroughly heated, stirring occasionally. Yield: about 2 cups.

*Glazed Leg of Lamb*

## GLAZED STUFFED LAMB

1 medium onion, chopped
¼ cup butter or margarine
2 cups soft breadcrumbs
3 tablespoons chopped fresh
  mint leaves
1½ teaspoons grated orange
  rind
1 egg, beaten
¾ teaspoon salt, divided
½ teaspoon pepper, divided
1 (5- to 6-pound) boneless leg
  of lamb roast
1 cup Chablis or other dry
  white wine
⅔ cup orange juice
Glaze (recipe follows)
Orange slices (optional)
Fresh mint leaves (optional)

Sauté onion in butter in a medium skillet until tender; add breadcrumbs, chopped mint, orange rind, egg, ½ teaspoon salt, and ¼ teaspoon pepper, stirring well. Set aside.

Spoon breadcrumb mixture into the opening formed by boning. Fold roast over breadcrumb mixture; tie securely with string. Place roast in a roasting pan. Sprinkle roast with remaining salt and pepper. Insert meat thermometer, if desired.

Bake, uncovered, at 350° for 30 minutes. Combine wine and orange juice; pour over roast. Bake for 1½ hours.

Score fat in a diamond design; coat with glaze. Bake until desired degree of doneness: 15 minutes or 140° (rare); 35 minutes or 160° (medium); 1 hour or 170° (well done).

Transfer roast to a warm serving platter; let stand 10 minutes before slicing.

Skim fat from pan drippings. Discard fat, and pour pan drippings over roast. Garnish with orange slices and mint leaves, if desired. Yield: 6 to 8 servings.

### Glaze:

¼ cup honey
1 tablespoon orange juice
2 tablespoons chopped fresh
  mint leaves

Combine all ingredients; stir well. Yield: about ¼ cup.

## STUFFED LEG OF LAMB

1 (5- to 5½-pound) boneless
  leg of lamb
1 tablespoon finely chopped
  onion
½ teaspoon salt
¼ teaspoon pepper
2 cups soft breadcrumbs
¼ cup butter or margarine,
  melted
2 tablespoons diced green
  chiles
1 teaspoon salt
½ teaspoon dried whole
  thyme
Dash of paprika
3 tablespoons all-purpose
  flour
½ teaspoon salt
¼ teaspoon pepper
1½ cups water

Remove the fell (tissue-like covering) from lamb with a sharp knife. Trim excess fat. Rub opening formed from boning with onion, ½ teaspoon salt, and ¼ teaspoon pepper.

Combine breadcrumbs, butter, chiles, 1 teaspoon salt, thyme, and paprika. Spoon into opening. Fold lamb over stuffing; fasten with skewers, and tie securely with string.

Dredge lamb in flour; sprinkle with ½ teaspoon salt and ¼ teaspoon pepper. Place in a shallow roasting pan. Pour water around lamb. Insert meat thermometer, if desired.

Bake, uncovered, at 400° for 30 minutes; reduce heat to 350°. Bake until desired degree of doneness: about 1 hour or 140° (rare); about 1½ hours or 160° (medium); about 2 hours or 170° (well done). Transfer lamb to a warm serving platter. Let stand 10 minutes before slicing. Yield: 6 to 8 servings.

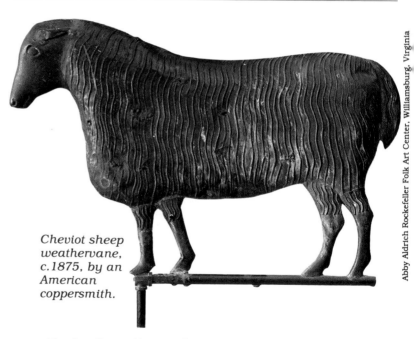

*Cheviot sheep weathervane, c.1875, by an American coppersmith.*

I n England, mutton is hung some time before cooking. There must be something in the air of England quite different from that of America in reference to the hanging of meats and game; there, it is to be confessed, the mutton, after having hung a certain length of time, certainly is most delicious; here it would be unwholesome, simply not fit to eat.

*Practical Cooking, and Dinner Giving,* Mary F. Henderson, 1877.

*Sheep graze in Mercer County, Kentucky.*

Photographic Archives,
University of Louisville

## ROASTED LAMB SHOULDER

1 (5- to 6-pound) lamb shoulder roast
1 clove garlic, halved
2 tablespoons olive oil
1 teaspoon salt, divided
¾ teaspoon coarsely ground black pepper, divided
2 cups water
1 tablespoon Worcestershire sauce
1 medium onion, chopped
2 tablespoons all-purpose flour

Remove the fell (tissue-like covering) from roast with a sharp knife. Rub surface of roast with garlic and olive oil; sprinkle with ¾ teaspoon salt and ½ teaspoon pepper. Place roast in a large Dutch oven; cover and bake at 350° for 1 hour, turning occasionally. Skim fat from pan drippings; discard fat.

Combine water, Worcestershire sauce, onion, remaining salt, and pepper; pour over roast. Cover and bake 1 hour or until tender.

Transfer roast to a warm serving platter, and keep warm. Reserve pan drippings.

Combine flour and small amount of water to form a smooth paste. Combine flour mixture and pan drippings in a small saucepan. Cook over medium heat, stirring constantly, until thickened and bubbly. Serve gravy with roast. Yield: 4 to 6 servings.

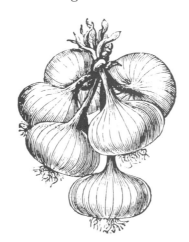

## LAMB POT ROAST

1 (3-pound) lamb shoulder roast
1 pound new potatoes, peeled and quartered
4 carrots, scraped and cut into 3-inch pieces
4 stalks celery, cut into 3-inch pieces
1 (14½-ounce) can tomatoes, undrained
3 cups water
1 tablespoon salt
1 teaspoon pepper

Remove the fell (tissue-like covering) from roast with a sharp knife. Place roast in a greased roasting pan. Arrange potatoes, carrots, and celery in pan. Combine remaining ingredients; pour over roast.

Cover and bake at 350° for 1½ hours. Uncover and continue baking for 30 minutes or until roast is tender, basting frequently with pan drippings.

Transfer roast and vegetables to a warm serving platter. Let roast stand 10 minutes before slicing. Yield: 4 servings.

# CHOPS AND SHANKS

## GRILLED LAMB CHOPS

4 (1-inch-thick) lamb
   rib chops
2 tablespoons butter or
   margarine, softened
1½ teaspoons chopped
   fresh parsley
½ teaspoon salt
Dash of pepper
Dash of paprika
1 teaspoon lemon
   juice

Trim excess fat from chops. Combine softened butter, parsley, salt, pepper, and paprika, mixing until smooth and creamy. Stir in lemon juice. Spread butter mixture evenly on both sides of chops.

Place chops on grill over medium coals. Grill chops 5 to 6 minutes on each side or until desired degree of doneness. Yield: 4 servings.

## BROILED LAMB RIBLETS

16 (¾-inch-thick) lamb
   rib chops
2 teaspoons salt
1 cup chili sauce
½ cup chopped onion
¼ cup orange juice
2 tablespoons honey
1 teaspoon prepared
   horseradish

Place chops in a deep container. Sprinkle with salt; add water to cover. Let stand 1 hour. Drain well. Place chops on rack in a shallow roasting pan.

Combine chili sauce, chopped onion, orange juice, honey, and horseradish, mixing well. Set mixture aside.

Place roasting pan 4 to 5 inches from heating element. Broil lamb chops 5 minutes on each side. Brush with chili sauce mixture; broil an additional 4 minutes on each side, basting frequently with sauce. Yield: 8 servings.

*Dapper salesman could not have come at a better time.*

For the most attractive presentation, rib bones of a crown roast or lamb chops should be "Frenched." With a sharp knife, scrape away meat and gristle to a uniform depth on each rib. For chops, clean bone a third of the way down toward meat. To decorate with frills, cut a 5- by 8-inch paper rectangle. Fold in half lengthwise. Cut through folded side at ⅛-inch intervals almost across. Reverse fold, bringing open edges together again. Roll the uncut edge, allowing enough to go around the bone one time and overlap. Secure roll with tape. Slip frills over bones at serving time.

## PLANKED LAMB CHOPS

8 (1-inch-thick) lamb rib chops
¼ cup butter or margarine
½ teaspoon salt
¼ teaspoon pepper
3 cups mashed potatoes
1 (10½-ounce) can asparagus spears, drained

Sauté chops in butter in a large skillet over medium heat 8 minutes on each side or until browned. Sprinkle chops on both sides with salt and pepper.

Place chops around edges of a large ovenproof platter. Spoon potatoes into center of platter; garnish with asparagus.

Place platter 5 to 6 inches from heating element. Broil chops and vegetables for 10 minutes or until potatoes are lightly browned. Yield: 6 to 8 servings.

## SAUTÉED LAMB CHOPS

4 (½-inch-thick) lamb rib chops
2 tablespoons brandy
½ teaspoon salt
1 egg yolk, beaten
½ cup all-purpose flour
¼ cup vegetable oil
¼ cup red currant jelly
⅛ teaspoon dry mustard

Brush chops on both sides with brandy, and sprinkle with salt. Brush chops on both sides with egg yolk; dredge in flour.

Sauté chops in oil in a heavy skillet over medium heat 4 minutes on each side or until golden brown. Drain. Set aside and keep warm.

Combine jelly and mustard in a saucepan. Cook over low heat, stirring constantly, until jelly melts. Spoon mixture over chops to serve. Yield: 2 servings.

## BREADED LAMB CHOPS

1 cup fine dry breadcrumbs
1 teaspoon salt
½ teaspoon pepper
6 (¾-inch-thick) lamb loin chops
2 eggs, beaten
¼ cup clarified butter

Combine breadcrumbs, salt, and pepper. Dip chops in egg; dredge in breadcrumb mixture.

Melt butter in a large skillet over medium heat. Add chops, and cook for 5 minutes, turning to brown both sides.

Transfer chops to a 13- x 9- x 2-inch baking dish. Cover and bake at 350° for 30 minutes or until chops are tender. Yield: 6 servings.

*Planked Lamb Chops. Once you find a plank, the rest is easy.*

*In* Tables for Ladies,
*Edward Hopper caught*
*an early 1900s scene:*
*Arranging fresh fruits in*
*a restaurant window.*

## LENA'S LAMB CHOPS AND PINEAPPLE

8 (½-inch-thick) lamb loin
  chops
½ teaspoon salt
¼ teaspoon white pepper
8 slices canned pineapple
Fresh parsley sprigs (optional)

Place chops in a large skillet.
Cook over medium heat until
chops are browned on both
sides. Sprinkle chops with salt
and pepper.

Place pineapple slices on rack
in a broiler pan; top pineapple
slices with browned chops.
Place broiler pan 5 inches from
heating element. Broil 10 minutes. Transfer chops and pineapple slices to a warm serving
platter. Garnish with parsley, if
desired, before serving. Yield: 4
servings.

## BAKED LAMB CHOPS

¼ cup plus 2 tablespoons fine
  dry breadcrumbs
2 teaspoons finely chopped
  onion
½ cup butter or margarine
1 teaspoon Worcestershire
  sauce
1 teaspoon salt
¼ teaspoon pepper
2 hard-cooked eggs
4 (1-inch-thick) lamb loin
  chops
Spiced peaches (optional)
Fresh parsley sprigs
  (optional)

Sauté breadcrumbs and
onion in butter in a small skillet
over medium heat until onion is
tender. Remove from heat, and
add Worcestershire sauce, salt,
and pepper; stir well. Set aside.

Slice eggs in half lengthwise,
and carefully remove yolks.
Press yolks through a sieve;
finely chop whites. Add yolks
and whites to stuffing mixture;
stir well.

Place 1 tablespoon stuffing
mixture on each chop. Place a 4-
x 4-inch square of aluminum
foil over stuffing. Turn chops
over, and repeat procedure.
Tightly wrap each chop in aluminum foil.

Place chops in a 13- x 9- x 2-
inch baking pan. Bake at 375°
for 1 hour. Unwrap chops, and
place on a warm serving platter.
Garnish with spiced peaches
and parsley sprigs, if desired.
Yield: 4 servings.

## BRAISED LAMB SHANKS

2 to 2½ pounds lamb shanks
1 tablespoon shortening
1 medium onion, chopped
½ cup chopped celery
½ cup catsup
½ cup water
1 clove garlic, minced
1½ teaspoons Worcestershire
  sauce
½ teaspoon salt
¼ teaspoon pepper

Trim shanks of excess fat.

Heat shortening in a large skillet; add shanks, and cook over medium heat until browned. Add onion, celery, catsup, water, garlic, Worcestershire sauce, salt, and pepper. Cover and simmer 1½ hours or until shanks are tender.

Transfer shanks to a warm platter. Yield: 4 servings.

## LAMB SHANKS BAKED IN FRUITED WINE

½ teaspoon salt
⅛ teaspoon pepper
1 cup all-purpose flour
2 to 2½ pounds lamb shanks
1 cup Burgundy or other dry
  red wine
1 (6-ounce) package dried
  apricots
1 cup pitted prunes
½ cup golden raisins
½ cup sugar
2 tablespoons vinegar
2 tablespoons lemon juice
2 tablespoons honey
½ teaspoon ground allspice
½ teaspoon ground cinnamon

Combine salt, pepper, and flour; mix well. Dredge shanks in flour mixture, coating well. Place shanks in a greased 2½-quart shallow baking dish.

Cover and bake at 350° for 1½ hours.

Combine remaining ingredients in a small Dutch oven; bring to a boil. Reduce heat; simmer 5 minutes, stirring frequently. Spoon sauce over shanks. Cover; bake at 400° for 30 minutes or until shanks are tender. Yield: 4 servings.

## BARBECUED LAMB SHANKS

2 to 2½ pounds lamb shanks
½ cup all-purpose flour
¼ cup shortening, melted
1 teaspoon salt
¼ teaspoon pepper
2 tablespoons firmly packed
  brown sugar
1 cup water
½ cup vinegar
¼ cup catsup
2 tablespoons Worcestershire
  sauce
1 medium onion, finely
  chopped
½ cup raisins
8 pitted prunes

Dredge lamb shanks in flour, coating well. Sauté shanks in shortening in a heavy skillet over medium heat until browned. Drain shanks on paper towels.

Place shanks in a lightly greased 2½-quart shallow baking dish. Sprinkle shanks with salt and pepper. Combine sugar, water, vinegar, catsup, Worcestershire sauce, onion, raisins, and prunes; mix well. Pour sauce mixture over shanks. Cover and bake at 300° for 2 hours or until shanks are tender. Yield: 4 servings.

*Braised Lamb Shanks.*
*The seasonings are exciting,*
*so prepare plenty of hot*
*rice to complement them.*

# SPECIAL WAYS WITH LAMB

## SHISH KABOBS

1 (5-pound) boneless leg of
  lamb, cut into 1½-inch
  cubes
1 cup port or other sweet red
  wine
½ cup vinegar
½ cup olive oil
2 tablespoons lemon juice
2 tablespoons chopped fresh
  parsley
2 teaspoons sugar
1 teaspoon dried whole
  oregano
1 teaspoon salt
½ teaspoon pepper
1 large onion, chopped
6 cloves garlic, minced
4 medium-size green peppers,
  seeded and cut into 1½-inch
  pieces
½ pound fresh mushrooms
1 (10-ounce) package pearl
  onions
1 pint cherry tomatoes
Hot cooked rice

Remove excess fat and fell (tissue-like covering) from lamb.

Combine next 11 ingredients
in a large shallow container.
Add lamb; cover and marinate
in refrigerator overnight.

Remove lamb from marinade;
discard marinade. Alternate
cubes of lamb with green pepper, mushrooms, pearl onions,
and tomatoes on skewers. Place
kabobs on grill about 5 inches
from medium coals. Grill 15 to
20 minutes, turning frequently.
Serve over hot cooked rice.
Yield: 8 to 10 servings.

*Shish Kabobs are good
for outdoor feasting.*

## GREEK LAMB WITH ZUCCHINI

1 cup chopped onion
1 clove garlic, minced
1 tablespoon chopped
  fresh parsley
2 tablespoons butter or
  margarine
2 pounds boneless leg of
  lamb, cubed
1 (14½-ounce) can tomatoes,
  undrained and chopped
½ cup water
½ teaspoon salt
¼ teaspoon dried mint
  flakes
⅛ teaspoon pepper
1½ pounds zucchini, cut
  into ½-inch-thick
  slices
2 tablespoons olive oil

Sauté onion, garlic, and parsley in butter in a large Dutch
oven until tender. Add lamb;
brown evenly on all sides. Stir in
tomatoes, water, salt, mint
flakes, and pepper. Cover and
simmer 30 minutes.

Brown zucchini slices on both
sides in hot oil in a large skillet.
Drain on paper towels. Add zucchini to lamb mixture. Cover
and simmer 5 minutes or until
zucchini is tender.

Transfer lamb and zucchini to
a warm serving platter, reserving pan liquid in Dutch oven.

Skim excess fat from pan liquid; discard fat. Bring pan liquid to a boil; reduce heat, and
simmer 5 minutes. Pour sauce
over lamb and zucchini. Yield: 4
to 6 servings.

## LAMB PILAF

1½ to 2 pounds lean lamb
  for stewing, cut into
  1½-inch cubes
1 medium onion, chopped
3 tablespoons vegetable oil
3 cups beef broth
1 (12-ounce) package pitted
  prunes, cooked, drained,
  and quartered
2 large green peppers,
  chopped
1 cup uncooked regular rice
4 (⅛-inch-thick) lemon
  slices
1 teaspoon salt
¼ teaspoon pepper
½ teaspoon ground oregano

Sauté lamb and onion in oil in a small Dutch oven over medium heat for 10 minutes, stirring frequently. Add beef broth; cover and simmer mixture for 20 minutes.

Remove from heat, and pour mixture into a greased 2½-quart casserole. Add remaining ingredients; stir well.

Cover and bake at 350° for 1 hour and 15 minutes. Uncover and bake an additional 10 minutes or until liquid is absorbed. Yield: 4 to 6 servings.

*Sunday morning at New Orleans' French Market, c.1867.*

## LAMB STEW

2½ pounds boneless leg of
  lamb, cubed
8 small potatoes, peeled
  and cut into
  ½-inch-thick slices
4 medium turnips, peeled
  and quartered
4 small onions, quartered
4 carrots, scraped and cut
  into 2-inch pieces
1 (10-ounce) package
  frozen green peas
1 (10-ounce) package
  frozen lima beans
4 cups water
1 teaspoon salt
½ teaspoon pepper

Place all ingredients in a large Dutch oven. Cover and cook over low heat 1½ hours or until meat is tender. Yield: about 4 quarts.

## CREOLE LAMB STEW

1 pound dried lima beans
2 tablespoons shortening
2 pounds lamb shoulder
  roast, cut into 1-inch cubes
2 teaspoons salt
½ teaspoon pepper
1 medium onion, chopped
6 stalks celery, coarsely
  chopped
2 (14½-ounce) cans tomatoes,
  undrained
¼ cup all-purpose flour
1 cup water

Sort and wash beans; place in a large Dutch oven. Cover with water 2 inches above beans; let soak overnight. Drain and rinse beans; set aside.

Melt shortening in a medium skillet; add lamb, and sauté over medium heat until browned.

Combine beans, lamb, salt, pepper, and onion with water to cover in a large Dutch oven. Bring to a boil; reduce heat. Cover and simmer 1 hour. Add celery and tomatoes; cook 30 minutes or until lamb is tender.

Remove lamb and vegetables with a slotted spoon, reserving pan liquid in Dutch oven. Set lamb and vegetables aside, and keep warm.

Combine flour and water, blending until smooth. Add to reserved pan liquid, blending well. Cook over medium heat, stirring frequently, until mixture is thickened. Stir in lamb and vegetables, mixing well. Serve immediately. Yield: about 3 quarts.

*Navajo Indians baking cornmeal bread, c.1949.*

## INDIAN STEW

2 pounds lamb shoulder
   steak, cut into 1-inch cubes
3 tablespoons vegetable oil
3½ cups water, divided
4 medium-size yellow squash,
   sliced
1 (15-ounce) can pinto beans,
   drained
1 (10-ounce) package frozen
   whole kernel corn
1 red pepper pod, halved and
   seeded
1 teaspoon salt
½ teaspoon pepper
¼ cup all-purpose flour

Cook lamb in oil in a large Dutch oven over medium heat until browned. Add 3 cups water, squash, pinto beans, corn, pepper pod, salt, and pepper. Bring to a boil. Reduce heat; cover and simmer 2 hours.

Combine remaining water and flour; stir until smooth. Pour into stew; cook, stirring frequently, until thickened and bubbly. Remove pepper pod; discard. Yield: about 8½ cups.

## NAVAJO STEW

1 pound dried pinto beans
2 to 2½ pounds boneless leg
   of lamb, cubed
2 medium onions, chopped
2 cloves garlic, minced
2 tablespoons vegetable oil
1 bay leaf
1 tablespoon chili powder
2 teaspoons salt
¼ teaspoon whole
   peppercorns
6 cups water
2 (14½-ounce) cans tomatoes,
   undrained and chopped
1 (15-ounce) can garbanzo
   beans, drained
1 (10-ounce) package frozen
   whole kernel corn
1 (10-ounce) package frozen
   green peas
4 carrots, scraped and sliced
4 potatoes, peeled and cubed
Tortillas

Sort and wash beans; place in a large Dutch oven. Cover with water 2 inches above beans; let soak overnight. Drain beans; set aside.

Brown lamb, onion, and garlic in hot oil in a large Dutch oven. Add pinto beans, bay leaf, chili powder, salt, peppercorns, and water. Bring to a boil. Reduce heat; cover and simmer for 1½ hours.

Add remaining ingredients except tortillas; simmer, uncovered, 1 hour or until vegetables and lamb are tender. Remove bay leaf and peppercorns; discard. Serve stew with tortillas. Yield: 4 quarts.

H aricot of mutton was a perennial favorite among the Southern planters. The term haricot, from the French word for kidney bean, came to mean a stew containing vegetables. There was a rich gravy, thickened with butter and brown flour. Haricots were made of veal and beef as well.

# RAGÔUT OF LAMB

1 tablespoon butter or
  margarine
¼ cup plus 3 tablespoons
  all-purpose flour
2 cups hot water
2 pounds lamb shoulder,
  cut into ½-inch
  cubes
1 large carrot, finely
  chopped
1 onion, finely chopped
3 whole cloves
¼ bay leaf
½ teaspoon minced fresh
  parsley leaves
1 teaspoon salt
¼ teaspoon white pepper
1 (10-ounce) package frozen
  green peas
Farina Balls

Melt butter in a small Dutch oven over low heat; add flour, stirring until smooth. Cook, stirring constantly, until mixture is golden brown. Gradually add water; cook over medium heat, stirring constantly, until thickened and bubbly. Add remaining ingredients, except peas and Farina Balls.

Cover and simmer 2½ hours or until lamb is tender. Add peas, and continue cooking 15 minutes. Remove cloves and bay leaf; discard. Serve ragôut with Farina Balls. Yield: about 2 quarts.

Farina Balls:

2 cups milk
1 cup regular cream of
  wheat (enriched farina)
½ teaspoon salt
2 egg yolks, beaten
⅔ cup crushed saltine
  crackers
Vegetable oil

Heat milk in top of a double boiler; add cream of wheat and salt. Cook 5 minutes or until mixture is thickened, stirring frequently. Cool.

Add egg yolks, mixing well. Shape into 1-inch balls; roll in cracker crumbs to coat. Deep-fry balls in hot oil (375°) until golden brown. Serve Farina Balls immediately with ragôut. Yield: 2 dozen.

# 1944 CRUSTLESS LAMB PIE

1½ pound lamb shoulder
  roast, cut into 1½-inch
  cubes
½ cup all-purpose flour
2 tablespoons bacon
  drippings
2 cups water
2½ teaspoons salt
¼ teaspoon pepper
1 (8½-ounce) can lima beans,
  drained
4 small onions, peeled
4 carrots, scraped and cut
  into ⅛-inch-thick slices
2 cups seasoned mashed
  potatoes

Dredge lamb in flour; coat well. Sauté lamb in drippings in a medium Dutch oven over medium heat until browned. Add water, salt, and pepper, stirring well; cover and cook over low heat 1½ hours.

Add lima beans, onions, and carrots; cover and continue cooking over low heat 30 minutes or until vegetables are tender.

Remove from heat, and spoon meat mixture into a lightly greased 2-quart casserole. Spoon mashed potatoes around edges of casserole.

Place casserole 5 to 6 inches from heating element. Broil 5 minutes or until potatoes are crusty brown. Yield: 6 servings.

*Note*: Mashed potatoes may be piped with a pastry bag for a more decorative effect.

*World War II poster shows Woman Ordnance Worker at work.*

*Wartime Lamb Pie in a pastry flavored with mint.*

## WARTIME LAMB PIE

2 pounds lamb shoulder
   steak, cut into 1-inch
   cubes
1 teaspoon salt
½ teaspoon pepper
2 tablespoons shortening
1 cup plus 3 tablespoons
   water, divided
1 cup sliced fresh
   mushrooms
2 tablespoons all-purpose
   flour
3 medium carrots, peeled
   and sliced into thin
   1½-inch strips
2 small onions, quartered
1 (10-ounce) package frozen
   green peas
Mint Pastry Shell
¼ cup butter or margarine,
   melted

Sprinkle lamb with salt and
pepper. Melt shortening in a
large skillet over medium heat.

Add lamb, and cook until
browned, stirring frequently.
Add 1 cup water and mush-
rooms; cover and simmer 30
minutes.

Combine remaining 3 tablespoons water and flour, stirring
until smooth. Pour flour mixture into lamb mixture; cook,
stirring frequently, until thickened and bubbly.

Cook carrots and onions in a
small amount of boiling salted
water until crisp-tender; drain
well. Cook peas according to
package directions; drain well.

Line cooked carrots upright
around edge of pastry shell. Fill
center of pastry with lamb mixture. Place peas and onions al-
ternately around lamb mixture.
Drizzle melted butter over vegetables. Serve immediately. Yield:
6 to 8 servings.

Mint Pastry Shell:
1½ cups all-purpose flour
½ teaspoon salt
½ cup shortening
¼ cup minced fresh mint
   leaves
3 tablespoons cold water

Combine flour and salt; cut in
shortening with a pastry
blender until mixture resembles
coarse meal. Stir in mint leaves.
Sprinkle water evenly over flour
mixture, and stir with a fork
until dry ingredients are moistened. Shape dough into a ball,
and chill 30 minutes.

Roll dough to ⅛-inch thickness on a floured surface. Line a
9-inch pieplate with pastry.
Prick bottom and sides of shell.
Bake at 425° for 12 minutes or
until lightly browned. Cool completely on a wire rack. Yield: one
9-inch pastry shell.

# A SAVORY LAMB PIE

Pastry for double crust
   10-inch deep-dish pie
½ teaspoon salt
¼ teaspoon pepper
⅛ teaspoon mace
⅛ teaspoon ground nutmeg
⅛ teaspoon ground cloves
1 (3- to 4-pound) leg of lamb
   roast, cut into 2-inch cubes
1 pound veal sweetbreads
1 (12-ounce) container fresh
   Select oysters, undrained
¼ cup plus 2 tablespoons
   butter or margarine, divided
¼ cup all-purpose flour
½ cup Madeira or other dry,
   sweet wine
1 egg yolk

Line a 10-inch deep-dish pie-plate with half of pastry; chill remaining pastry.

Sprinkle salt, pepper, mace, nutmeg, and cloves over lamb cubes. Place lamb cubes in a medium Dutch oven; cover with water, and simmer 2 hours or until lamb is tender. Drain lamb, reserving broth. Set lamb and broth aside.

Cover sweetbreads with cold water, and let soak 1 hour; drain. Place in a Dutch oven, and cover with fresh cold water. Cover and simmer 1 hour. Drain well, and chop; set aside.

Drain oysters, reserving ⅓ cup liquid. Cover oysters with water, and cook over medium heat 8 to 10 minutes or until edges of oysters curl; set aside.

Add reserved lamb broth to oyster liquid to equal 2 cups; discard remaining lamb broth.

Melt ¼ cup butter in a heavy saucepan over low heat; add flour, stirring until smooth. Cook 1 minute, stirring constantly. Gradually add lamb broth mixture. Cook over medium heat, stirring constantly, until thickened and bubbly. Remove from heat.

Combine wine and egg yolk, stirring until well blended. Slowly add wine mixture to creamed broth mixture, stirring gently to form a sauce. Combine lamb, sweetbreads, oysters, and sauce in a large mixing bowl; stir well. Spoon mixture evenly into pastry shell, and dot with remaining 2 tablespoons butter. Cover with top crust, and slit in several places to allow steam to escape; seal and flute edges. Cover edges of pie with aluminum foil, and bake at 350° for 1 hour and 10 minutes. Yield: 8 to 10 servings.

# LAMB PATTIES WITH TOMATO GRAVY

2 (14½-ounce) cans whole
   tomatoes, undrained
1 pound ground lamb
2 cups mashed potatoes
1 medium onion, finely
   chopped
1 teaspoon salt
¼ cup all-purpose flour
¼ cup vegetable oil
Tomato Gravy

Drain and chop tomatoes; reserve 1½ cups juice for Tomato Gravy. Combine tomatoes, lamb, potatoes, onion, and salt; mix well. Shape into 2-inch patties; dredge in flour.

Heat vegetable oil in a large skillet; add lamb patties. Cook over medium heat until browned on one side; turn and brown other side. Transfer patties to a warm serving platter. Reserve 2 tablespoons pan drippings for Tomato Gravy. Serve lamb patties with Tomato Gravy. Yield: about 2 dozen.

Tomato Gravy:

2 tablespoons all-purpose
   flour
2 tablespoons reserved pan
   drippings
1½ cups reserved tomato
   juice
1 tablespoon chopped fresh
   parsley

Combine flour with reserved pan drippings in a large skillet; blend until smooth. Cook 1 minute, stirring constantly. Gradually add reserved tomato juice; cook over medium heat, stirring constantly, until thickened and bubbly. Stir in parsley. Yield: about 1½ cups.

# SHEPHERD'S PIE

1½ pounds ground lamb
1 egg, beaten
½ cup milk
½ cup soft breadcrumbs
½ cup diced, cooked
   carrots
¼ cup chopped onion
½ teaspoon salt
5 cups seasoned mashed
   potatoes

Cook lamb in a large skillet over medium heat until browned, stirring to crumble meat. Drain well. Combine lamb, egg, milk, breadcrumbs, carrots, onion, and salt in a large bowl, mixing well.

Press half of potatoes firmly into a lightly greased 9-inch pie-plate. Spoon lamb mixture over potatoes. Spread remaining potatoes evenly over top. Bake at 350° for 1 hour or until top is lightly browned. Yield: 6 to 8 servings.

## PASTITSIO

1 (8-ounce) package elbow
  macaroni
¼ cup plus 2 tablespoons
  butter or margarine,
  divided
2 pounds ground lamb
2 small onions, chopped
3 cloves garlic, minced
2 (16-ounce) cans whole
  tomatoes, undrained and
  chopped
½ teaspoon ground oregano
½ teaspoon ground nutmeg
⅛ teaspoon ground
  cinnamon
3 eggs, beaten
¾ cup Parmesan cheese,
  divided
1 large eggplant, peeled and
  cut into ¼-inch-thick slices
Olive oil
3 tablespoons all-purpose
  flour
3½ cups warm milk
½ teaspoon salt
¼ teaspoon pepper
4 eggs, beaten
1 (15-ounce) carton ricotta
  cheese

Cook macaroni according to
package directions; drain well,
and set aside.

Melt 3 tablespoons butter in a
large Dutch oven. Add lamb,
onion, and garlic; cook, stirring
frequently, until vegetables are
tender. Drain off pan drippings;
discard.

Add tomatoes, oregano, nutmeg, and cinnamon to Dutch
oven. Simmer, uncovered, 40
minutes or until liquid has
evaporated; cool.

Add 3 eggs, ½ cup Parmesan
cheese, and macaroni, mixing
well. Spread macaroni mixture
into a lightly greased 13- x 9- x
2-inch baking dish.

Brush both sides of eggplant
with olive oil. Place on a baking
sheet; broil 5 minutes on each
side or until golden brown.
Layer eggplant slices over macaroni mixture; sprinkle with remaining ¼ cup Parmesan
cheese.

Melt remaining 3 tablespoons
butter in a heavy saucepan over
low heat; add flour, stirring
until smooth. Cook 1 minute,
stirring constantly. Gradually
add milk, salt, and pepper, stirring constantly, until thickened
and bubbly. Remove from heat.

Gradually stir one-fourth of
hot mixture into 4 eggs; add to
remaining hot mixture, stirring
constantly. Add ricotta cheese;
blend well. Pour over eggplant-
macaroni mixture. Bake at 325°
for 45 minutes. Let stand 10
minutes before serving. Yield:
10 servings.

## SPRINGTIME LAMB RING

2 pounds ground lamb
1 cup milk
1 cup crushed saltine
  crackers
1 egg
1 medium-size green pepper,
  seeded and finely chopped
2 tablespoons finely chopped
  onion
1½ teaspoons salt
½ teaspoon pepper
1 (10-ounce) package frozen
  green peas
6 small new potatoes, cooked
  and peeled

Combine first 8 ingredients;
mix well. Spoon mixture into an
oiled, ovenproof 6-cup ring
mold. Bake at 350° for 1 hour.
Carefully drain excess grease
from mold. Unmold onto a warm
serving platter.

Cook peas according to package directions. Fill center of ring
with peas and potatoes. Yield: 6
to 8 servings.

## LAMB HASH

2 tablespoons butter or
  margarine
3 cups cooked roast lamb, cut
  into ½-inch cubes
1 teaspoon salt, divided
½ teaspoon pepper
½ teaspoon garlic salt
¼ teaspoon savory
2 tablespoons all-purpose
  flour
1 (16-ounce) can tomatoes,
  undrained
6 potatoes, cut into 1-inch
  cubes
2 cups boiling water
Toast points

Melt butter in a large Dutch
oven; add lamb, ½ teaspoon
salt, pepper, garlic salt, and savory. Sauté over medium heat
until lamb is browned.

Add flour; blend until smooth.
Add tomatoes and potatoes.
Cover; simmer 20 minutes over
low heat. Add water; cover and
cook 20 minutes. Add remaining salt; stir well. Serve over
toast points. Yield: 6 cups.

*The taste must have been heavenly! Package label mid-1800s.*

SUPERIOR AURORA BRAND QUALITY

*Macaroni*

Collection of Business Americana

# PINEAPPLE-MINT LAMB RING

2 cups diced, cooked lamb
½ cup chopped onion
1 (8-ounce) bottle commercial French dressing
2 envelopes unflavored gelatin
¼ cup water
1 cup unsweetened pineapple juice
⅓ cup vinegar
⅓ cup water
¼ cup sugar
¼ teaspoon salt
3 ripe olives, sliced
¼ teaspoon peppermint extract
2 drops green food coloring
Lettuce leaves
Fresh mint leaves

Combine lamb, onion, and French dressing in a shallow dish; cover and marinate at least 1 hour.

Combine gelatin and ¼ cup water in a large mixing bowl; stir to soften gelatin. Set aside.

Combine pineapple juice, vinegar, ⅓ cup water, sugar, and salt in a small saucepan. Bring to a boil. Remove from heat; pour over gelatin. Stir until gelatin dissolves. Pour one-fourth of gelatin mixture into a lightly oiled 3½-cup ring mold. Chill until partially set.

Arrange olive slices around ring over gelatin. Chill until set.

Pour one-half remaining gelatin mixture into mold. Chill until set.

Drain lamb; discard marinade. Spoon lamb over gelatin in mold.

Combine remaining gelatin mixture, peppermint extract, and food coloring. Spoon over lamb in mold. Chill until firm. Invert onto a lettuce-lined platter. Garnish center with mint leaves. Yield: 6 servings.

*Pineapple-Mint Lamb Ring is a pretty main dish salad.*

# LAMB CURRY

1¾ cups diced celery
1½ cups diced onion
1 large apple, peeled and diced
¼ cup butter or margarine
3 tablespoons all-purpose flour
2 cups hot water
1 teaspoon brown bouquet sauce
2 cups cooked roast lamb, cut into ½-inch cubes
½ cup raisins
2 teaspoons curry powder
½ teaspoon salt
⅛ teaspoon pepper
⅛ teaspoon ground cloves
Hot cooked rice
Condiments

Sauté celery, onion, and apple in butter in a large Dutch oven over medium heat until onion is golden brown. Stir in flour.

Combine water and bouquet sauce; gradually add to sautéed mixture, blending until smooth. Add next 6 ingredients, mixing well. Bring mixture to a boil; reduce heat. Cover and simmer 30 minutes or until mixture is thickened and bubbly.

Serve over hot cooked rice with the following condiments: (about ¾ cup each) chutney, flaked coconut, chopped hard-cooked egg, crumbled cooked bacon, and salted peanuts. Yield: 4 to 6 servings.

# VARIETY MEATS

## A Tribute to Our Evolving Taste

Conscientious mothers still push liver, and Ris de Veau holds its place on the menus of the better French restaurants, but that makes only two fingers needed to count today's usage of the variety meats once so widely used in the South. Not enough of us live in the Southwest to know the delights of Son-of-a-Gun Stew which was once a staple on cattle drives.

Time was, when cold weather brought slaughtering time, waste simply was not in the Southerner's lexicon. Liver, heart, sweetbreads, kidneys, brains . . . all fed the families involved in the labor of meat preparation. Since old cookbooks unashamedly presented recipes for every possible part of a meat animal, it would be wrong to think that these variety meats were eaten exclusively by the indigent and servants, most of whom could not read.

While it is true that some plantation masters instructed that the "offal" be given the laborers, men like Jefferson served "Calf's head, boiled with a sharp vinegar sauce and calves' liver, larded and stuffed, with a sauce." For William Byrd, master of Westover, tongue was a welcome dish.

Mary Randolph, the high-born Virginian of cookbook fame, put oysters with sweetbreads in a pie, and she grilled calf's head, garnishing it with brain cakes and broiled sweetbreads. She fricasseed calves' feet and made rennet from the calf's stomach.

The art of making dessert gelatin from animal feet was perfected years before Randolph put recipes on paper. Four calves' feet, she said, would make 2 quarts of jelly. The feet were boiled, and the liquid degreased and clarified. Flavoring was wine or lemon, sugar, and spices. Such "jellies" were featured at all the best houses.

So when — and why — did we become so finicky? Perhaps the dishes represented in this chapter deserve more than a cursory glance.

*Son-of-a-Gun Stew, traditional noon dinner at round-up time, still has its adherents. Spanish in origin, it was picked up by early Texas cattlemen from their Mexican neighbors.*

*1800s mustard ad.*

## BAHAMA KIDNEYS IN RED WINE

1 (½- to 1-pound) beef kidney
2 cups water
3 tablespoons apple cider
    vinegar
¼ cup all-purpose flour
1 teaspoon salt
¼ teaspoon pepper
½ cup chopped onion
1 clove garlic, minced
3 tablespoons butter or
    margarine
⅛ teaspoon ground thyme
1 bay leaf
⅔ cup beef broth
½ cup Burgundy or other
    dry red wine
Hot cooked noodles

Remove and discard any fatty tissue from kidney. Combine water and vinegar; soak kidney in water-vinegar mixture 1 hour. Drain well.

Slice kidney in ¼-inch-thick slices. Combine flour, salt, and pepper; dredge kidney in flour mixture. Set aside.

Sauté onion and garlic in butter in a large skillet over medium heat. Add kidney; cook over low heat 5 minutes or until browned, turning occasionally. Add thyme, bay leaf, beef broth, and wine; cover and simmer 30 minutes or until kidney is tender. Remove and discard bay leaf. Serve over hot cooked noodles. Yield: 4 servings.

## BRAINS IN SHERRY SAUCE

2 pounds veal brains
3 tablespoons all-purpose
    flour
1 tablespoon dry mustard
1 teaspoon salt
1 teaspoon pepper
2 cups finely chopped
    onion
1 cup finely chopped
    green pepper
3 tablespoons olive oil
1 cup half-and-half, divided
¼ cup Parmesan cheese
¼ cup plus 2 tablespoons
    sherry
Toast points (optional)

Wash brains thoroughly in cold water; carefully remove membrane. Drain well.

Combine flour, mustard, salt, and pepper; dredge brains in flour mixture, coating well. Set aside.

Sauté onion and green pepper in hot oil in a large Dutch oven until tender. Add brains, and cook until browned, turning gently to brown all sides.

Gradually add ½ cup half-and-half. Cover and cook over low heat 40 minutes. Combine remaining half-and-half, Parmesan cheese, and sherry. Pour over brains mixture; cook an additional 5 minutes over low heat. Serve immediately over toast points, if desired. Yield: 6 to 8 servings.

# STEAK AND KIDNEY PUDDING

¼ pound lamb kidneys
Suet crust (recipe follows)
1½ pounds boneless round
  steak, cut into ½-inch cubes
2 tablespoons all-purpose
  flour
½ teaspoon salt
¼ teaspoon pepper
1 small onion, finely chopped
3 tablespoons water

Place kidneys with water to cover in a medium bowl; let stand 1 hour. Drain. Remove center cord and excess fat from kidneys; discard. Cut kidneys into small pieces, and set aside.

Roll two-thirds of pastry to ⅛-inch thickness, and fit into a 1-quart casserole.

Combine kidneys, steak, flour, salt, and pepper; toss lightly to coat well. Add onion; mix well.

Spoon steak mixture into pastry-lined casserole; sprinkle with water. Cover with top crust, and slit in several places to allow steam to escape; seal and flute edges.

Place casserole in a shallow baking pan of hot water. Cover pan with greased aluminum foil. Steam pudding at 350° for 3½ hours, replacing water in baking pan as needed. Yield: 6 servings.

*Note:* For a brown crust, remove aluminum foil and pan of water. Place casserole on rack 3 to 4 inches from heating element. Broil 3 minutes or until pastry is golden brown.

Suet Crust:

2 cups all-purpose
  flour
2 teaspoons baking
  powder
½ teaspoon salt
¼ pound beef suet, finely
  chopped
¼ cup plus 2 tablespoons
  cold water

Combine flour, baking powder, and salt; cut in suet with a pastry blender until mixture resembles coarse meal. Sprinkle cold water evenly over surface; stir with a fork until dry ingredients are moistened. Shape dough into a ball; chill. Yield: pastry for one double-crust 1-quart pudding.

*Steak and Kidney Pudding, suet-crusted, steamed, and ever so English. Brown it if you like.*

## KIDNEY PIE

1 pound lamb kidneys
1 beef-flavored bouillon
  cube
1 cup boiling water
1 small onion, chopped
2 tablespoons all-purpose
  flour
¼ cup cold water
1 cup cubed, cooked potatoes
½ cup sliced, cooked carrots
½ teaspoon salt
¼ teaspoon pepper
Baking Powder Biscuits

Place kidneys and water to cover in a heavy saucepan; let stand 1 hour. Drain. Remove center cord and excess fat from kidneys; discard. Cut kidneys into small pieces.

Combine kidney, bouillon cube, boiling water, and onion in a medium saucepan. Bring to a boil. Reduce heat, and simmer 15 minutes.

Combine flour and cold water, stirring well to form a smooth paste. Stir into kidney mixture. Cook over medium heat, stirring constantly, until thickened and bubbly.

Stir in potatoes, carrots, salt, and pepper. Remove from heat; spoon into a 9-inch pieplate. Top with Baking Powder Biscuits. Bake at 400° for 15 minutes or until biscuits are golden brown. Yield: 6 to 8 servings.

**Baking Powder Biscuits:**

1½ cups all-purpose flour
1 tablespoon baking powder
¼ teaspoon salt
¼ cup shortening
¼ cup plus 2 tablespoons
  milk

Combine flour, baking powder, and salt; stir well. Cut in shortening with a pastry blender until mixture resembles coarse meal. Sprinkle milk evenly over flour mixture, stirring until dry ingredients are moistened.

Turn dough out onto a lightly floured surface; knead lightly 10 to 12 times. Roll dough to ½-inch thickness; cut with a 1½-inch biscuit cutter. Yield: 18 biscuits.

In 17th- and 18th-century England, the choicest (and not so choice) parts of game offal were called "umbles." In his diary, Pepys once complained that he had been fed "umble pie, the meanest dinner." The poor man's standby of old England was later up-graded and presented to society as steak and kidney pie. Hence the origin of our expression "to eat humble pie." Since we all must eat humble pie at one time or another, it is nice to know what is in it.

## SAUTÉED LIVER WITH AVOCADO

1½ pounds thinly sliced
  calves' liver
½ cup butter, divided
2 medium-size ripe avocados
½ cup chicken broth,
  undiluted
⅓ cup dry white vermouth
¼ cup lemon juice
1 tablespoon freeze-dried
  chives
1 teaspoon minced fresh
  parsley

Sauté liver in 2 tablespoons butter in a large skillet over medium heat 5 minutes on each side. Remove liver to a warm serving platter.

Cut avocados into ¼-inch-thick lengthwise slices. Sauté slices in 2 tablespoons butter over medium heat 1 minute on each side or until avocado is slightly soft. Arrange slices around liver on platter.

Combine remaining ¼ cup butter, chicken broth, vermouth, lemon juice, chives, and parsley in a small saucepan. Bring to a boil. Remove sauce from heat; serve over liver and avocado. Yield: 6 servings.

## SMOTHERED LIVER AND ONIONS

1 pound thinly sliced calves'
  liver
½ teaspoon salt
¼ teaspoon pepper
¼ cup all-purpose flour
2 medium onions, thinly
  sliced
¼ cup bacon drippings
1 cup water

Sprinkle liver with salt and pepper; dredge in flour. Set aside.

Sauté onions in hot bacon drippings in a large skillet until tender. Remove onions, reserving bacon drippings in skillet.

Cook liver in drippings over medium heat until browned on both sides; top with onion slices. Add water. Cover; simmer 20 minutes or until liver is no longer pink.

Transfer liver and onion slices to a warm serving platter; pour pan liquid over top. Serve immediately. Yield: 4 servings.

*Smothered Liver and Onions, sure way to many a man's heart.*

# MARYLAND BAKED LIVER

3 slices bacon
1 medium onion, chopped
3 whole cloves
1 clove garlic, minced
2 tablespoons chopped fresh
  parsley
Pinch of dried whole savory
Pinch of dried marjoram
  leaves
Pinch of dried whole thyme
1 pound thinly sliced calves'
  liver
¼ teaspoon salt
¼ teaspoon pepper
⅛ teaspoon red pepper
¼ cup beef broth
1 tablespoon all-purpose flour
¼ cup Madeira or other sweet
  wine
Chopped fresh parsley

Cook bacon in a large skillet until crisp; remove from skillet, reserving drippings. Crumble bacon, and set aside.

Sauté onion, cloves, garlic, 2 tablespoons parsley, and spices in bacon drippings until onion is tender. Remove and discard cloves.

Place liver in a 10- x 6- x 2-inch baking dish. Spoon onion mixture evenly over liver; sprinkle with bacon, salt, and pepper. Add beef broth. Cover with aluminum foil; bake at 350° for 45 minutes. Transfer liver to a warm serving platter; reserve pan drippings.

Combine flour and a small amount of water to form a smooth paste. Stir into reserved pan drippings. Add wine. Cook over medium heat, stirring constantly, until thickened and bubbly. Pour gravy over liver. Sprinkle with chopped parsley. Yield: 4 servings.

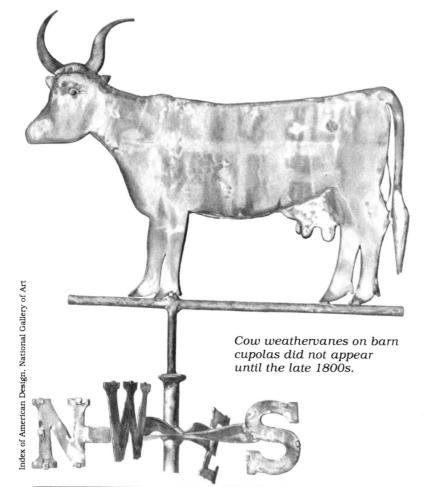

*Cow weathervanes on barn cupolas did not appear until the late 1800s.*

# GRILLED CALVES' LIVER

4 (1½-inch-thick) slices
  calves' liver
1 teaspoon salt
½ teaspoon pepper
4 slices bacon
½ cup butter or margarine,
  melted
½ cup shortening,
  melted
1 teaspoon garlic powder

Sprinkle liver with salt and pepper. Wrap each piece of liver with a slice of bacon; secure with a wooden pick.

Combine butter, shortening, and garlic powder, stirring well. Place liver on grill 4 to 5 inches from heat. Grill over medium coals 20 minutes or until tender, turning liver every 5 minutes. Baste frequently with sauce. Yield: 4 servings.

# CALVES' LIVER IN SOUR CREAM

4 slices bacon
1 pound thinly sliced
  calves' liver
1 medium onion,
  chopped
1 (8-ounce) carton
  commercial sour cream
½ cup sliced fresh
  mushrooms
½ teaspoon salt
½ teaspoon pepper
Paprika

Cook bacon in a large skillet until crisp. Remove from skillet, reserving bacon drippings. Drain bacon on paper towels. Set bacon aside.

Sauté liver and onion in reserved bacon drippings 5 minutes. Combine sour cream, mushrooms, salt, and pepper; add to liver mixture, stirring gently, until well combined. Cover and bake at 325° for 30 minutes.

Transfer liver to a warm serving platter. Spoon pan liquid over liver. Top with bacon slices, and sprinkle with paprika. Yield: 4 servings.

*Fresh meat stall in the city market of Savannah, c.1911.*

## BAKED LIVER IN CREOLE SAUCE

1 pound thinly sliced
   calves' liver
½ teaspoon salt
¼ teaspoon pepper
¼ cup all-purpose flour
3 tablespoons bacon
   drippings
1 medium onion, chopped
1 medium-size green pepper,
   chopped
1 clove garlic, minced
3 tablespoons all-purpose
   flour
1 (8-ounce) can tomato
   sauce
1 cup water
1 bay leaf
½ cup (2 ounces) shredded
   Cheddar cheese

Sprinkle liver with salt and pepper; dredge in flour. Brown liver on both sides in hot bacon drippings in a large skillet. Remove liver to a 10- x 6- x 2-inch baking dish, reserving pan drippings in skillet.

Sauté onion, green pepper, and garlic in pan drippings. Add flour, tomato sauce, water, and bay leaf. Bring to a boil, stirring constantly. Remove from heat; pour over liver.

Bake, uncovered, at 325° for 30 minutes. Remove and discard bay leaf. Sprinkle with cheese; bake an additional 10 minutes or until cheese melts. Yield: 4 servings.

Calf fries, sometimes called "mountain oysters," were considered a delicacy by cattlemen when it was time to castrate the young bulls in the herd to make steers of them. They would throw the "oysters" on the fire used for heating the branding irons and then eat them roasted and salted. Lamb fries are on the menus of the best restaurants in Lexington's Bluegrass area, which is famous for Kentucky spring lamb.

*Turn-of-the-century housewife tends kettle of dumplings.*

## LIVER AND DUMPLINGS

1 pound thinly sliced
  calves' liver
¼ teaspoon salt
⅛ teaspoon pepper
⅓ cup all-purpose flour
¼ cup shortening
1 large onion, sliced
¼ cup all-purpose flour
3 cups water
Dumplings (recipe follows)

Sprinkle liver with salt and pepper; dredge in ⅓ cup flour.

Melt shortening in a large skillet over medium heat; brown liver on both sides. Remove and keep warm, reserving pan drippings in skillet.

Sauté onion in pan drippings until tender. Stir in ¼ cup flour; cook 1 to 2 minutes. Gradually add water, stirring constantly, until mixture is thickened and bubbly. Return liver to skillet. Cover and simmer 5 minutes.

Prepare dumplings. Drop dumpling batter by tablespoonfuls into liver and gravy mixture. Cover and simmer 5 minutes. Turn dumplings; cover and simmer 5 additional minutes. Serve immediately. Yield: 6 servings.

### Dumplings:

1 cup all-purpose flour
2 teaspoons baking powder
½ teaspoon salt
⅓ cup milk
1 egg
2 tablespoons vegetable
  oil

Combine flour, baking powder, and salt; stir well. Add milk, egg, and oil, stirring until dry ingredients are moistened. Yield: 12 dumplings.

## LIVER NIPS

¾ pound ground chuck
¾ pound thinly sliced calves'
  liver
1 medium onion, quartered
¾ cup all-purpose flour
½ teaspoon salt
¼ teaspoon pepper

Place meat and liver in a Dutch oven with water to cover; bring to a boil. Cover; reduce heat to low, and simmer 15 minutes. Remove from heat; drain well, reserving broth in a heavy saucepan.

Grind ground chuck and liver with a meat grinder, using the finest blade. Add onion; grind a second time.

Combine meat mixture, flour, salt, and pepper; mix well. Stir in ¼ cup reserved broth. Bring remaining broth to a boil. Drop mixture by tablespoonfuls into boiling broth, allowing room for expansion. Cover; reduce heat, and simmer 12 minutes. Remove liver nips from broth to a warm serving platter. Repeat procedure with remaining meat mixture. Yield: about 3 dozen appetizer servings.

## SWEETBREADS WRAPPED IN BACON

1 pound veal sweetbreads
12 slices bacon, cut
  in half

Place sweetbreads in a medium mixing bowl; cover with cold water. Set aside to soak for 1 hour. Drain well; remove and discard white membrane.

Place sweetbreads and water to cover in a small Dutch oven. Bring to a boil. Reduce heat, and simmer 20 minutes. Drain well, and rinse with cold water.

Cool sweetbreads completely.

Cut sweetbreads into 24 bite-size pieces. Wrap a half slice of bacon around each piece of sweetbread, and secure with a wooden pick.

Sauté sweetbreads in a large skillet over medium heat until bacon is crisp and brown. Remove sweetbreads from skillet, and drain well on paper towels. Serve immediately. Yield: 24 appetizer servings.

## BROILED SWEETBREADS WITH LEMON SAUCE

2 pounds veal sweetbreads
2½ tablespoons lemon juice,
  divided
1¼ teaspoons salt, divided
¼ cup butter
1 tablespoon chopped fresh
  parsley
½ teaspoon onion juice
⅛ teaspoon pepper

Place sweetbreads in a medium mixing bowl; cover with cold water. Set aside to soak for 1 hour. Drain well; remove and discard white membrane.

Place sweetbreads, 1½ tablespoons lemon juice, 1 teaspoon salt, and water to cover in a small Dutch oven. Bring to a boil. Reduce heat, and simmer 20 minutes. Drain well, and rinse with cold water. Cool sweetbreads completely.

Slice sweetbreads in half lengthwise; place on a well-greased rack in a shallow roasting pan. Broil 5 to 6 inches from heating element for 8 minutes. Transfer sweetbreads to a warm serving platter. Set aside.

Combine remaining 1 tablespoon lemon juice, ¼ teaspoon salt, butter, parsley, onion juice, and pepper in a small saucepan. Bring mixture to a boil, stirring well. Remove sauce from heat, and pour over sweetbreads. Serve immediately. Yield: 6 servings.

*Sweetbreads Wrapped in Bacon: a flavor change from the bacon-wrapped oyster, chicken liver, or water chestnut.*

"It is usually necessary to bespeak sweetbreads several days in advance," wrote Marion Harland in *Breakfast, Luncheon and Tea*, 1877, "as they are both scarce and popular." She went on to give recipes for two brown fricassees, one white one; sweetbreads larded and stewed, sweetbreads larded and fried; sweetbreads broiled, roasted, and sautéed au vin. This delicacy of previous centuries is viewed now in a paradoxical way: In some exclusive markets, one really must bespeak sweetbreads in advance, but in others, they are regarded as offal and sold in bulk for use by those seeking cheaper meat.

## BREADED SWEETBREADS

1 cup all-purpose flour
1 cup beer
1 pound veal sweetbreads
½ cup saltine cracker
  crumbs
Vegetable oil
½ teaspoon salt

Combine flour and beer; cover and set aside for 1½ hours.

Place sweetbreads in a medium mixing bowl; cover with cold water. Set aside to soak for 1 hour. Drain well; remove and discard white membrane.

Place sweetbreads and water to cover in a small Dutch oven. Bring to a boil. Reduce heat, and simmer 20 minutes. Drain well, and rinse with cold water. Cool sweetbreads completely.

Slice sweetbreads in half lengthwise. Dip in beer batter; roll in cracker crumbs. Deep fry in hot oil (375°) until golden brown. Drain on paper towels, and sprinkle with salt. Serve immediately. Yield: 4 servings.

## SAUTÉED SWEETBREADS WITH GRAVY

1 pound veal sweetbreads
3 cups water
1 cup chopped celery leaves
1 small onion, quartered
1½ teaspoons salt, divided
½ teaspoon pepper, divided
1 cup all-purpose flour
¼ cup butter or margarine

Place sweetbreads in a medium mixing bowl; cover with water. Set aside to soak for 1 hour. Drain well; remove and discard white membrane.

Combine sweetbreads, water, celery leaves, onion, 1 teaspoon salt, and ⅛ teaspoon pepper in a medium Dutch oven. Bring to a boil. Cover; reduce heat, and simmer 30 minutes.

Remove sweetbreads, and cut into serving-size pieces; set aside. Strain broth, and reserve 1 cup. Discard vegetables and remaining broth.

Combine flour and remaining salt and pepper. Dredge sweetbreads in flour; set aside.

Melt butter in a skillet over medium heat. Add sweetbreads; cook over low heat 10 minutes or until browned, turning as necessary. Remove sweetbreads; drain. Reserve pan drippings. Transfer sweetbreads to a warm serving platter.

Pour reserved 1 cup broth into pan drippings. Cook over medium heat, stirring frequently, until thickened and bubbly. Serve gravy with sweetbreads. Yield: 4 servings.

## SWEETBREADS DELUXE

2 to 3 pounds veal
  sweetbreads
2 tablespoons lemon juice
1½ teaspoons salt, divided
¼ cup butter or margarine
½ cup sherry
⅛ teaspoon white pepper
⅛ teaspoon onion powder
¾ cup whipping cream
2 tablespoons flour
¼ cup water
Toast points
Paprika

Place sweetbreads in a large mixing bowl; cover with cold water. Set aside to soak for 1 hour. Drain well; remove and discard white membrane.

Place sweetbreads and water to cover in a medium Dutch oven. Add lemon juice and 1 teaspoon salt. Bring to a boil. Reduce heat, and simmer 20 minutes. Drain well, and rinse with cold water. Cool completely. Slice sweetbreads into 1-inch slices; set aside.

Melt butter in a heavy skillet over medium heat. Add sweetbreads; cook slowly for 10 minutes or until browned. Add sherry, pepper, onion powder, and remaining salt; cover and simmer 5 minutes. Add cream; simmer 15 minutes.

Combine flour and ¼ cup water; stir until smooth. Add flour mixture to sweetbreads mixture; simmer until thickened, stirring occasionally. Spoon over toast points; sprinkle with paprika, and serve. Yield: 8 servings.

*A 1908 poster depicts a General Electric toaster as a welcome appliance in a well-appointed home.*

## SHERRIED SWEETBREADS IN PASTRY SHELLS

1 pound veal sweetbreads
2 tablespoons butter or margarine, divided
2 tablespoons all-purpose flour, divided
2 cups half-and-half, divided
½ pound fresh mushrooms, sliced
¼ cup chopped almonds, toasted
¼ cup sherry
¼ teaspoon nutmeg
¼ teaspoon salt
⅛ teaspoon pepper
12 baked 3-inch pastry shells
½ cup (2 ounces) Cheddar cheese

Place sweetbreads in a medium mixing bowl; cover with cold water. Set aside to soak for 1 hour. Drain well; remove and discard white membrane.

Place sweetbreads and water to cover in a small Dutch oven. Bring to a boil. Reduce heat, and simmer 20 minutes. Drain well, and rinse with cold water. Cool completely. Chop sweetbreads, and set aside.

Melt 1 tablespoon butter in a saucepan over low heat; add 1 tablespoon flour, stirring until smooth. Gradually add 1 cup half-and-half; cook over medium heat, stirring constantly, until thickened. Set aside.

In a medium skillet, melt remaining butter; add mushrooms, and sauté until tender. Add remaining flour, stirring until smooth. Cook 1 minute, stirring constantly. Gradually add remaining half-and-half. Cook over medium heat, stirring constantly, until sauce is thickened and bubbly.

Combine reserved cream sauce and mushroom sauce. Add sweetbreads, almonds, sherry, nutmeg, salt, and pepper. Cook over low heat until heated; stir occasionally.

Spoon mixture into pastry shells; sprinkle with cheese. Place pastry shells on a lightly greased baking sheet. Bake at 375° for 5 minutes or until cheese melts. Yield: 12 servings.

*Oysterman's haul fills the deck: Chesapeake Bay, Maryland.*

## SWEETBREAD AND OYSTER PIE

1 pound veal sweetbreads
2 tablespoons butter or margarine
2 tablespoons all-purpose flour
1 cup half-and-half
1 teaspoon salt
¼ teaspoon pepper
1 9-inch double crust pastry
1 (12-ounce) container fresh Select oysters, drained
1 tablespoon milk

Place sweetbreads in a medium mixing bowl; cover with cold water. Set aside to soak for 1 hour. Drain well; remove and discard white membrane.

Place sweetbreads and water to cover in a small Dutch oven. Bring to a boil. Reduce heat, and simmer 30 minutes. Drain well, and rinse with cold water. Cool completely. Cut into bite-size pieces. Set aside.

Melt butter in a heavy saucepan over low heat; add flour, and stir until smooth. Cook 1 minute, stirring constantly. Gradually add half-and-half; cook over medium heat, stirring constantly, until thickened and bubbly. Stir in salt and pepper.

Roll half of pastry to ⅛-inch thickness, and fit into a 9-inch pieplate. Layer oysters and sweetbreads in pastry shell. Pour sauce over oysters and sweetbreads. Cover with top crust, and slit in several places to allow steam to escape; seal and flute edges. Brush with milk. Bake at 350° for 40 minutes or until golden brown. Yield: 6 servings.

## PICKLED TONGUE

1 (2- to 2½-pound) beef
  tongue
6 whole cloves
3 peppercorns
2 bay leaves
1 tablespoon vinegar
2 tablespoons salt

Scrub tongue thoroughly with a stiff brush, and rinse well with cold water. Place tongue in a large Dutch oven. Add water to cover. Bring to a boil; reduce heat. Cover and simmer 1 hour.

Add remaining ingredients; cover and simmer 2½ hours or until tongue is tender. Remove tongue from broth, and plunge into cold water. Remove and discard skin from tongue. Chill tongue thoroughly. Cut into ¼-inch-thick slices to serve. Yield: 6 servings.

## SWEET-AND-SOUR TONGUE

2 tablespoons baking soda
2 tablespoons plus 1¼
  teaspoons salt, divided
1 (2- to 2½-pound) beef
  tongue
2 tablespoons butter or
  margarine
2 tablespoons all-purpose
  flour
¼ cup sugar
¼ teaspoon pepper
2 bay leaves
½ cup chopped onion
¼ cup vinegar

Combine soda and 2 tablespoons salt; rub over surface of tongue. Scrub with a stiff brush; rinse with cold water.

Place tongue and 1 teaspoon salt in a large Dutch oven; add water to cover. Bring to a boil; reduce heat. Cover; simmer 3 hours or until tender.

Remove tongue from broth, and plunge into cold water. Reserve 1 cup broth. Remove and discard skin from tongue. Cut tongue into ½-inch-thick slices.

Place butter in a heavy saucepan. Cook over low heat until golden brown. Add flour; stir until smooth. Cook 1 minute, stirring constantly. Gradually add reserved 1 cup broth; cook over medium heat, stirring constantly, until thickened.

Stir in ¼ teaspoon salt, and remaining ingredients. Add sliced tongue, and simmer, uncovered, 30 minutes. Discard bay leaves.

Place tongue on warm platter and serve with pan liquid. Yield: 6 to 8 servings.

*Enjoy Pickled Tongue in a combination sandwich.*

## GERMAN TONGUE WITH RAISIN SAUCE

1 (2- to 2½-pound) beef tongue
2 stalks celery, halved
1 medium onion, quartered
1 teaspoon salt
2 tablespoons butter or margarine
2 tablespoons all-purpose flour
2 tablespoons wine vinegar
2 tablespoons sugar
½ cup raisins

Scrub tongue with a stiff brush; rinse well with cold water. Place tongue in a large Dutch oven. Add celery, onion, salt, and water to cover. Bring to a boil; reduce heat. Cover; simmer 3½ hours or until tender.

Remove tongue from broth, and plunge into cold water. Strain broth, reserving 1½ cups. Remove and discard skin from tongue. Cut tongue into ¼-inch-thick slices.

Melt butter in a heavy saucepan over low heat; add flour, and stir until smooth. Cook 1 minute, stirring constantly. Gradually add reserved broth; cook over medium heat, stirring constantly, until thickened and bubbly. Add vinegar, sugar, and raisins; cook 5 minutes.

Add sliced tongue; cook an additional 10 minutes or until sauce is thickened. Transfer tongue to a warm serving dish. Pour raisin sauce over tongue to serve. Yield: 6 to 8 servings.

Olla Podrida is the meat and vegetable stew known as the national dish of Spain. In Marion Harland's *Breakfast, Luncheon and Tea*, 1877, her recipe for Ollapodrida (one word) begins: "The sweetbreads, liver, heart, kidneys, and brains of a lamb. (Your butcher can easily procure all with timely notice.)" She then outlines a stew that's astonishingly close to "Son-of-a-Gun," especially as she ends with this note: "You can make a larger stew — or fry — of calf's sweetbreads, liver, heart, and brains, and by most people this would be relished more than the lamb ollapodrida." Interesting that Harland, who had traveled in Europe, should have written of Olla Podrida at about the same time the Texas cattlemen were getting the hang of Sun-of-a-Gun Stew, tutored as they were by their Spanish-Mexican neighbors.

## BREADED TRIPE

1 (24-ounce) can tripe, drained and rinsed
1 egg, beaten
1 tablespoon milk
¾ cup fine dry breadcrumbs
3 tablespoons shortening
Salt and pepper to taste

Cut tripe into serving-size pieces. Combine egg and milk in a small bowl; mix well. Dip tripe pieces in egg mixture. Dredge each piece in breadcrumbs.

Melt shortening in a large heavy skillet over medium heat. Fry tripe until golden brown on each side. Drain on paper towels. Sprinkle with salt and pepper; serve immediately. Yield: 4 servings.

## SON-OF-A-GUN STEW

1 pound veal sweetbreads
½ pound veal brains
¼ pound beef suet
1½ pounds veal kidneys, cut into small pieces
1 pound veal heart, cut into small pieces
1 pound calves liver, cut into small pieces
2 cups beef broth
1 large onion, chopped
1 (14½-ounce) can tomatoes, undrained and chopped
3 drops hot sauce
Salt to taste

Place sweetbreads and brains in a medium mixing bowl; cover with cold water. Set aside to soak for 1 hour. Drain well; remove and discard membranes. Chop brains, and set aside.

Place sweetbreads and water to cover in a small Dutch oven. Bring to a boil. Reduce heat, and simmer 20 minutes. Drain well, and rinse with cold water. Cool completely. Chop; set aside.

Heat beef suet in a large Dutch oven over low heat until crisp. Remove beef suet, and discard; reserve beef suet drippings in Dutch oven.

Add kidney, heart, and liver to Dutch oven. Cook over medium heat until browned, stirring occasionally. Add sweetbreads, brains, beef broth, onion, tomatoes, hot sauce, and salt to taste. Simmer, uncovered, 1½ hours or until meats are tender. Yield: 2 quarts.

*"The Old Cow Puncher," an authentic cowboy pictured in the middle of a meal.*

# SAUCES & GRAVIES

## The Ultimate Complement to Every Meat

G ravy, in the beginning, was understood to be the liquid that accumulated in the container placed on the hearth under meat as it roasted before the fire. The meat was continually basted with a rag dipped into the drippings. At the strategic moment, the final basting was administered, and the meat was lightly dredged with flour (frothed) and allowed to form a brown, bubbly crust. Not enough flour fell into the dripping pan to form gravy as we now think of thickened gravy. Sometimes the cook skimmed off some of the fat, but not always; grease was appreciated more then than it is now.

At last the term gravy, as used in recipes, came to mean rich, defatted broth. "Grease," declaimed Harland in *Breakfast, Luncheon, and Tea*, 1877, "is not gravy. . . . If you have no gravy ready, make it. Crack up bones from which you have cut the flesh, and [cook] with the refuse bits of meat, gristle, skin, etc.; cover with cold water and stew gently until you have extracted all the nourishment . . . from 2 cups of liquid, you have 1 cup of tolerable gravy . . . a little good gravy is a desideratum."

Sauces, usually quite simple, were important in the South's early years. Scraped horseradish was prescribed to sauce roast meats, except for lamb and mutton, when a sauce of onion or chopped mint and vinegar was recommended. Sorrel or parsley, stewed in butter, was also widely used as sauce. By 1800, sauces had taken on some sophistication; Jefferson and other world travelers are due some of the credit, for they brought back European sauce recipes. Many of our present-day sauces stem directly from them.

Southern cooks make no secret of the fact that gravy, well made, is a basic food; perhaps that is why we need such quantities of rice and biscuits to soak it up. We brown our flour to deepen flavor and use broth instead of water when possible, for, as Harland said, good gravy *is* a desideratum.

*Stages in sauce-making: Brown Stock (top), easily made at home and frozen, is used to make Basic Brown Sauce which, in turn, is an ingredient in Madeira Sauce (center) and Bordelaise Sauce (front).*

*Sites and Ames' meat market at Christmastime, Memphis, 1893.*

## SAUCE BÉARNAISE

½ cup Chablis
2 tablespoons tarragon vinegar
3 tablespoons chopped green onion
2 sprigs fresh parsley, chopped
1 teaspoon dried whole tarragon
¼ teaspoon cracked black pepper
3 egg yolks
½ cup butter or margarine, melted
2 teaspoons lemon juice
¼ teaspoon salt
2 dashes red pepper

Combine first 6 ingredients in a saucepan. Cook over medium heat 10 minutes or until liquid is reduced to ⅓ cup. Strain; discard vegetables and spices. Cool slightly.

Beat egg yolks until thick and lemon colored. Gradually stir one-fourth of hot mixture into yolks; add to remaining hot mixture, stirring constantly. Cook, stirring constantly, until thickened. Remove from heat; stir in butter, one tablespoon at a time. Stir in remaining ingredients. Serve sauce warm with beef tenderloin. Yield: 1 cup.

## SAUCE AU BEURRE NOIR

½ cup plus 2 tablespoons butter
3 tablespoons tarragon vinegar
½ teaspoon salt
¼ teaspoon pepper

Cook butter in a saucepan over low heat until golden brown; stir frequently. Stir in remaining ingredients. Serve sauce warm with sweetbreads. Yield: about ¾ cup.

## SAUCE BÉCHAMEL

1 small onion, finely chopped
1 tablespoon butter
1 tablespoon all-purpose flour
1 cup milk
½ teaspoon salt
⅛ teaspoon white pepper

Sauté onion in butter in a small saucepan over low heat until tender. Add flour; stir well. Cook 1 minute, stirring constantly. Gradually add milk; cook over low heat, stirring constantly, until thickened and bubbly. Add salt and pepper; stir well. Serve sauce hot with sweetbreads or as a base for other sauces. Yield: 1 cup.

# BASIC BROWN STOCK

3 pounds beef short ribs
3 pounds veal breast ribs
1 large onion, coarsely chopped
1 large carrot, scraped and cut into 2-inch pieces
4 quarts water
3 stalks celery, cut into 2-inch pieces
3 sprigs fresh parsley
2 teaspoons salt
4 whole peppercorns
3 whole cloves
1 bay leaf
¼ teaspoon dried whole thyme

Place ribs, onion, and carrot in a shallow roasting pan. Bake at 400° for 30 minutes or until meat is browned, turning to brown all sides.

Transfer ribs, onion, and carrots to a large stock pot. Add remaining ingredients. Bring mixture to a boil; reduce heat, and simmer, uncovered, for 3 hours. Remove from heat; let cool to lukewarm.

Strain stock, reserving liquid. Discard ribs, vegetables, and spices. Place stock liquid in a container; cover and refrigerate until thoroughly chilled. Lift solid fat from top of stock; discard fat. Use Basic Brown Stock as a base for soups, sauces, or gravies. Yield: about 3 quarts.

*Note*: Basic Brown Stock may be frozen up to 3 months.

# BASIC BROWN SAUCE

¼ cup butter or margarine
¼ cup all-purpose flour
2 cups Basic Brown Stock
⅛ teaspoon salt
⅛ teaspoon pepper

Melt butter in a medium saucepan; add flour, blending well. Cook, stirring constantly, until mixture has browned. Gradually add Basic Brown Stock; cook over medium heat, stirring constantly, until thickened and bubbly. Stir in salt and pepper. Serve sauce hot with roast beef or steak. Yield: about 2 cups.

# MADEIRA SAUCE

2 cups Basic Brown Sauce
½ cup Madeira

Simmer Basic Brown Sauce in a medium saucepan 20 minutes or until sauce has been reduced to 1 cup. Add Madeira; continue cooking 5 minutes. Serve sauce hot with roast beef or steak. Yield: about 1½ cups.

# BORDELAISE SAUCE

1 cup Burgundy
2 tablespoons minced shallots
⅛ teaspoon salt
Dash of ground thyme
½ bay leaf
1 cup Basic Brown Sauce
2 teaspoons chopped fresh parsley

Combine first 5 ingredients in a medium saucepan; simmer 20 minutes or until mixture is reduced to ⅓ cup. Strain mixture, reserving liquid; discard spices. Combine liquid and Basic Brown Sauce; simmer 10 minutes. Add parsley. Serve sauce hot with roast beef or steak. Yield: about 1 cup.

*Handsome Glenwood stove: 1922 women's magazine advertisement.*

## MUSHROOM SAUCE

½ cup sliced fresh
  mushrooms
1 tablespoon butter or
  margarine
1 cup Basic Brown Sauce
¼ cup sherry
1½ tablespoons finely
  chopped green onion
⅛ teaspoon salt
⅛ teaspoon pepper

Sauté mushrooms in butter
until tender; add Basic Brown
Sauce, sherry, onion, salt, and
pepper, stirring well. Simmer 5
minutes, stirring frequently.
Serve hot with roast beef or
steak. Yield: about 1¼ cups.

## JARDINIÈRE SAUCE

2 medium onions, chopped
1 clove garlic, minced
1 medium carrot, scraped
  and cut into 2-inch
  pieces
1 stalk celery, chopped
½ cup pan drippings from
  beef or veal roast
½ cup all-purpose flour
4½ cups beef broth, diluted
  and divided
1 bay leaf
Pinch of dried whole thyme
⅓ cup Madeira or other
  sweet wine
¼ cup tomato sauce

Sauté onion, garlic, carrot,
and celery in pan drippings in a
large saucepan over low heat
until vegetables are tender. Add
flour; cook over medium heat,
stirring constantly, 5 minutes
or until roux is the color of a
copper penny. Gradually add 3
cups broth, stirring until well
blended. Stir in bay leaf and
thyme. Cook, uncovered, over
medium heat 15 minutes.

Add remaining 1½ cups
broth; cook an additional 20
minutes, stirring occasionally.

Add wine and tomato sauce;
cook 5 minutes. Strain sauce
through a sieve; discard vegetables and bay leaf. Serve sauce
hot with roast beef or veal. Yield:
about 6 cups.

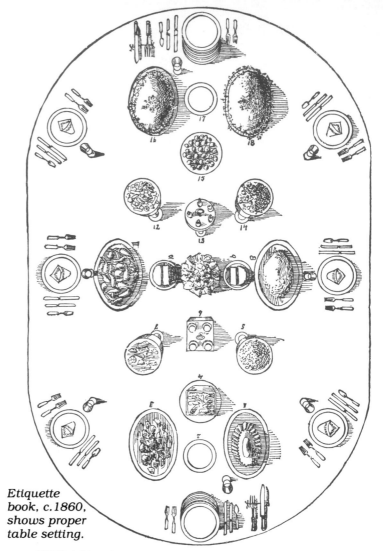

*Etiquette book, c.1860, shows proper table setting.*

## STEAK BUTTER

½ clove garlic
½ cup butter or margarine
1 teaspoon minced chives
¼ teaspoon ground savory
¼ teaspoon basil
¼ teaspoon ground marjoram
¼ teaspoon hickory salt
¼ teaspoon salt
⅛ teaspoon pepper
1 teaspoon lemon juice
Dash of hot sauce

Rub inside of bowl with garlic;
discard garlic. Add butter; beat
until light and fluffy. Add remaining ingredients, mixing
well. Store in a covered container in refrigerator until ready
to use. Serve Steak Butter at
room temperature on hot steak.
Yield: ½ cup.

## BARBECUE SAUCE

½ cup butter or margarine
2 tablespoons finely chopped
  onion
1 medium-size green pepper,
  finely chopped
4 lemon slices
1 whole dill pickle, finely
  chopped
1 cup vinegar
2 tablespoons Worcestershire
  sauce
2 tablespoons chili sauce
1 teaspoon firmly packed
  brown sugar

Place all ingredients in a medium saucepan. Bring to a boil;
reduce heat, and simmer 30
minutes. Use sauce for barbecuing beef, pork, or chicken. Yield:
about 2 cups.

## CREOLE BARBECUE SAUCE

2 cups water
2 cups vinegar
½ cup butter or margarine
¼ cup sugar
¼ cup catsup
¼ cup Worcestershire sauce
1 large red onion, chopped
6 stalks celery, chopped
1 lemon, thinly sliced
1 bay leaf
2 tablespoons red pepper
2 tablespoons celery seed
1 tablespoon salt
1 teaspoon pepper
1 teaspoon dry mustard
1 teaspoon garlic salt
2 drops hot sauce

Place all ingredients in a large Dutch oven, mixing well. Bring to a boil; reduce heat, and simmer 30 minutes, stirring occasionally. Use sauce for barbecuing beef, pork, or chicken. Yield: 2 quarts.

## LBJ'S BARBECUE SAUCE

1 clove garlic, minced
¼ cup butter or margarine
¼ cup vinegar
¼ cup catsup
¼ cup lemon juice
¼ cup Worcestershire sauce
½ teaspoon salt
⅛ teaspoon black pepper
⅛ teaspoon red pepper
2 drops hot sauce

Sauté garlic in butter in a small saucepan over low heat 5 minutes. Add remaining ingredients; stir well. Bring mixture to a boil; reduce heat, and simmer 20 minutes. Use sauce for barbecuing beef, pork, or chicken. Yield: ¾ cup.

## HENRY BANE STEAK SAUCE

1 cup catsup
½ cup chutney
½ cup Worcestershire sauce
1½ teaspoons hot sauce

Combine all ingredients, stirring well. Cover and chill. Serve sauce with steaks or roast beef. Yield: 2 cups.

## TANGY MARINADE SAUCE

1 cup vegetable oil
½ cup vinegar
2 tablespoons lemon juice
2 tablespoons finely chopped onion
1 clove garlic, minced
2 bay leaves
2 tablespoons marjoram leaves
1 teaspoon salt
1 teaspoon pepper

Combine all ingredients in a medium mixing bowl, and mix well. Use sauce as a marinade for steaks. Yield: about 2 cups.

## SOUR CREAM AND CHIVE SAUCE

½ cup commercial sour cream
¼ cup mayonnaise
1 tablespoon minced shallots
1 tablespoon chopped chives
1 tablespoon chopped fresh parsley
½ teaspoon prepared mustard
¼ teaspoon salt
⅛ teaspoon pepper
⅛ teaspoon hot sauce
Paprika

Combine sour cream, mayonnaise, shallots, chives, parsley, mustard, salt, pepper, and hot sauce, stirring well. Sprinkle with paprika. Serve sauce with cold sliced roast lamb. Yield: about ¾ cup.

*Appropriately dressed Lyndon Baines Johnson dips into Texas barbecue, 1947.*

## HORSERADISH SAUCE

1 cup whipping cream
2 tablespoons prepared
  horseradish
1 tablespoon tarragon vinegar
½ teaspoon salt
¼ teaspoon pepper
1 teaspoon prepared mustard
¼ teaspoon onion juice
¼ teaspoon hot sauce

Beat whipping cream until just thickened. Add remaining ingredients, mixing well; chill sauce at least 3 hours. Serve sauce cold with roast beef. Yield: about 2 cups.

## HORSERADISH-MUSTARD SAUCE

1 cup mayonnaise
2 tablespoons prepared
  horseradish
2 tablespoons horseradish
  mustard
2½ teaspoons sugar

Combine all ingredients, mixing well. Chill. Serve sauce with spiced round or roast beef. Yield: 1⅓ cups.

## HORSERADISH AND SOUR CREAM SAUCE

½ cup prepared horseradish
½ cup commercial sour
  cream
1 tablespoon plus 1 teaspoon
  vinegar
2 teaspoons sugar
1 teaspoon salt
½ teaspoon pepper

Combine all ingredients; stir well. Cover and chill. Serve with roast beef. Yield: 1 cup.

## TOMATO SAUCE

2 (14½-ounce) cans tomatoes,
  undrained
1 (¼-inch-thick) slice onion
8 whole cloves
2 tablespoons butter or
  margarine
2 tablespoons all-purpose
  flour

Combine tomatoes, onion, and cloves in a saucepan. Cook over medium heat 10 minutes or until onion is tender. Remove from heat; set aside.

Melt butter in a heavy saucepan over low heat; add flour, stirring until smooth. Cook 1 minute, stirring constantly. Add reserved tomato mixture; cook 2 minutes over medium heat, stirring occasionally. Strain mixture through a sieve; discard vegetables and spices. Serve sauce hot with veal cutlets or chops. Yield: 2¼ cups.

*Tomatoes are prominent in so many of our sauces that it is a shame they aren't all as large as the "Beefsteak."*

## SWEET-AND-SOUR TOMATO SAUCE

1 (6-ounce) can tomato paste
⅔ cup water
¼ cup vinegar
2 tablespoons brown sugar
1 tablespoon minced onion
1 teaspoon Worcestershire sauce
½ teaspoon garlic powder

Combine all ingredients in a small saucepan; simmer, stirring frequently, until thoroughly heated. Serve sauce hot with veal cutlets or chops. Yield: 1⅔ cups.

## MEXICAN SAUCE

1 small onion, chopped
1 medium-size green pepper, chopped
1 clove garlic, minced
2 tablespoons butter or margarine
2 tablespoons all-purpose flour
2 to 3 teaspoons chili powder
½ teaspoon salt
1 cup peeled, chopped tomatoes
½ cup beef broth
Hot sauce (optional)

Sauté onion, green pepper, and garlic in butter in a large skillet until tender. Add flour, chili powder, and salt; stir until smooth. Cook 1 minute, stirring constantly. Add tomato and beef broth; cook over medium heat, stirring constantly, until thickened and bubbly. Stir in hot sauce, if desired. Serve sauce hot with roast beef, steaks, meat loaf, or cold meats. Yield: about 2 cups.

## SPANISH SAUCE

2 tablespoons finely chopped green pepper
2 tablespoons finely chopped mushroom
1 teaspoon minced onion
¼ teaspoon salt
½ cup water
1 tablespoon butter
1 tablespoon all-purpose flour
1 teaspoon beef extract
½ cup beef broth
½ cup tomato juice
2 tablespoons chopped pimiento-stuffed olives
1 tablespoon Worcestershire sauce

Combine green pepper, mushroom, onion, salt, and water in a small saucepan. Bring to a boil. Reduce heat, and cook over low heat 20 minutes. Strain; set vegetables and reserved liquid aside.

Melt butter in top of a double boiler over medium heat; add flour, and cook 1 minute, stirring constantly. Gradually add reserved vegetable liquid, beef extract, beef broth, and tomato juice, blending until smooth. Add reserved vegetables, olives, and Worcestershire sauce. Cook over medium heat 10 minutes or until sauce is thickened and bubbly, stirring frequently. Serve sauce hot with roast beef. Yield: about 1 cup.

## SPICY FRUIT SAUCE

1 (16-ounce) jar pineapple preserves
1 (10-ounce) jar apple jelly
1 (1.12-ounce) can dry mustard
2 to 3 tablespoons prepared horseradish

Combine all ingredients in container of an electric blender; process at high speed for 2 minutes or until smooth. Cover and chill thoroughly. Serve sauce with cold roast beef, veal, or lamb. Yield: 2 cups.

## PIQUANT RELISH

2 small onions, finely chopped
1 tablespoon butter or margarine
1 tablespoon beef broth
2 whole dill pickles, finely chopped
1 teaspoon tarragon vinegar
½ teaspoon garlic salt
⅛ teaspoon salt
Dash of pepper
Pinch of red pepper

Sauté onion in butter in a small saucepan over low heat until tender. Add beef broth, pickle, vinegar, garlic salt, salt, and pepper; stir well. Bring to a boil; reduce heat, and simmer 5 minutes. Serve relish hot or cold with pickled tongue or cold roast beef. Yield: 1½ cups.

## MINT SAUCE

1 cup sugar
½ cup vinegar
2 tablespoons finely chopped fresh mint leaves

Combine sugar and vinegar in a medium saucepan; bring to a boil. Cook over high heat 5 minutes, stirring occasionally. Remove from heat; add mint leaves. Cover and let stand 5 minutes. Serve sauce hot with roast lamb. Yield: about ¾ cup.

## TANGY MINT SAUCE

½ cup chili sauce
½ cup mint jelly
1 tablespoon Worcestershire
  sauce
1 tablespoon prepared
  horseradish
2 teaspoons prepared
  mustard
¼ cup pan drippings from
  roast of lamb

Combine all ingredients in a heavy saucepan. Bring to a boil. Reduce heat; simmer 10 minutes. Serve sauce hot with roast lamb. Yield: about 1½ cups.

## JALAPEÑO JELLY

¾ cup ground, seeded
  jalapeño peppers
¾ cup ground green pepper
1¼ cups vinegar
6½ cups sugar
2 (3-ounce) packages liquid
  fruit pectin

Combine peppers, vinegar, and sugar in a large Dutch oven. Bring to a boil. Reduce heat; simmer, uncovered, 5 minutes. Add fruit pectin, mixing well. Bring to a boil. Reduce heat, and simmer 4 minutes.

Quickly pour jelly into sterilized jars, leaving ½-inch headspace; cover at once with metal lids, and screw bands tight. Process in a boiling-water bath 5 minutes. Serve jelly with beef, veal, or lamb. Yield: 6 half-pints.

*Spiced Port Wine Sauce brings out the subtle flavor of lamb.*

## SPICED PORT WINE SAUCE

¾ cup port or other sweet
  red wine
1 tablespoon sugar
1 teaspoon whole cloves
1 stick cinnamon, broken in
  half
Peel of 1 lemon
1 (12-ounce) jar red currant
  jelly

Combine wine, sugar, cloves, cinnamon, and lemon peel in a small saucepan. Bring to a boil; reduce heat, and simmer 15 minutes.

Strain mixture, discarding spices and lemon peel. Return strained wine mixture to saucepan. Stir in jelly. Simmer 1 to 2 minutes, stirring occasionally. Serve sauce warm with roast lamb. Yield: 1½ cups.

## ROAST PAN GRAVY

¼ cup plus 2 tablespoons fat
  from roast of beef
¼ cup plus 2 tablespoons
  all-purpose flour
Pan drippings from roast
  of beef
Water
Salt and pepper to taste

Combine fat and flour in a heavy skillet; stir until smooth. Cook, stirring constantly, over medium heat until browned.

Combine pan drippings and water to equal 3 cups. Gradually add pan drippings mixture to skillet; cook over medium heat, stirring constantly, until thickened and bubbly. Stir in salt and pepper. Serve hot with roast beef. Yield: about 3 cups.

## MUSHROOM PAN GRAVY

½ cup sliced fresh
  mushrooms
2 tablespoons butter or
  margarine
2 tablespoons all-purpose
  flour
1 cup beef broth
¼ teaspoon salt
⅛ teaspoon pepper
Dash of Worcestershire sauce
Dash of ground nutmeg

Sauté mushrooms in butter in a small saucepan over low heat 5 minutes. Add flour, stirring until mushrooms are well coated. Cook 1 minute, stirring constantly. Gradually add beef broth; cook over medium heat, stirring constantly, until thickened and bubbly. Stir in remaining ingredients. Serve with hamburgers, meat loaf, or steaks. Yield: about ¾ cup.

*A fanciful way to advertise beef extract, late 1800s: A sleek bovine attended by loving guardians.*

## CREAM GRAVY

2 tablespoons pan drippings
  from roast of beef
2 tablespoons all-purpose
  flour
1 cup milk
¼ teaspoon salt
⅛ teaspoon pepper

Heat drippings in a heavy saucepan over low heat. Add flour; stir until smooth. Cook 1 minute, stirring constantly. Gradually add milk; cook over medium heat, stirring constantly, until thickened. Add salt and pepper. Serve hot with roast beef. Yield: about 1 cup.

This advisory from *The Virginia Housewife* applies even to this day: "There should always be a supply of brown flour kept in readiness to thicken brown gravies, which must be prepared in the following manner: put a pint of flour in a Dutch oven, with some coals under it; keep constantly stirring it until it is uniformly of a dark brown, but none of it burnt, which would look like dirt in the gravy."

Collection of Business Americana

LIBBY, McNEILL & LIBBY,

# CUTS OF BEEF

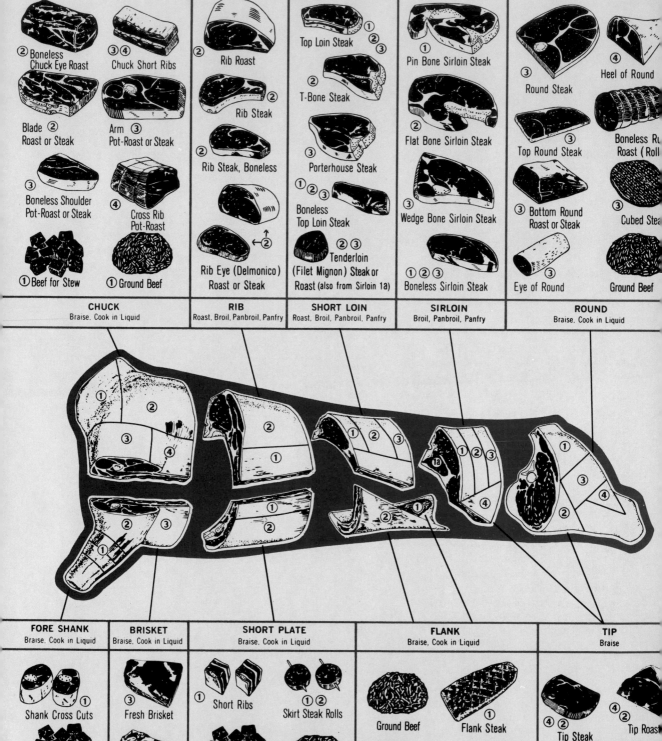

## CHUCK
Braise. Cook in Liquid

② Boneless Chuck Eye Roast
③④ Chuck Short Ribs
② Blade Roast or Steak
③ Arm Pot-Roast or Steak
③ Boneless Shoulder Pot-Roast or Steak
④ Cross Rib Pot-Roast
① Beef for Stew
① Ground Beef

## RIB
Roast, Broil, Panbroil, Panfry

② Rib Roast
② Rib Steak
② Rib Steak, Boneless
←②
② Rib Eye (Delmonico) Roast or Steak

## SHORT LOIN
Roast, Broil, Panbroil, Panfry

①②③ Top Loin Steak
② T-Bone Steak
③ Porterhouse Steak
①②③ Boneless Top Loin Steak
②③ Tenderloin (Filet Mignon) Steak or Roast (also from Sirloin 1a)

## SIRLOIN
Broil, Panbroil, Panfry

① Pin Bone Sirloin Steak
② Flat Bone Sirloin Steak
③ Wedge Bone Sirloin Steak
①②③ Boneless Sirloin Steak

## ROUND
Braise. Cook in Liquid

③ Round Steak
④ Heel of Round
③ Top Round Steak
③ Bottom Round Roast or Steak
③ Eye of Round
Boneless Ru Roast (Roll
③ Cubed Stea
Ground Beef

## FORE SHANK
Braise. Cook in Liquid

① Shank Cross Cuts
② Beef for Stew (also from other cuts)

## BRISKET
Braise. Cook in Liquid

③ Fresh Brisket
③ Corned Brisket

## SHORT PLATE
Braise. Cook in Liquid

① Short Ribs
①② Skirt Steak Rolls
①② Beef for Stew (also from other cuts)
② Ground Beef

## FLANK
Braise. Cook in Liquid

Ground Beef
① Flank Steak
Beef Patties
① Flank Steak Rolls

## TIP
Braise

④② Tip Steak
④② Tip Roas
④② Tip Kabobs

© National Live Stock and Meat Bo

# GOOD TO KNOW

## SELECTING QUALITY MEAT

Meat varies in tenderness according to the cut; however, all meat can be made tender by proper cooking. When selecting a cut of meat, keep the cooking method in mind. Consider not only the size and kind of cut, but also the quality of the meat.

- Check all meat for freshness and quality before purchasing. Read the label to determine the grade, cut, and weight.

- Beef is graded according to the quality of the meat: prime, choice, and good.

- Quality beef should be red in color, smooth in texture with an outside rim of creamy, firm fat. Prime and choice beef have streaks of internal fat (marbling) that add tenderness and flavor to the meat. Good beef is naturally less tender than prime or choice but, if cooked correctly, is just as flavorful and less expensive.

- When selecting veal, remember that color is the best indication of quality and freshness. Quality veal should be pink in color with no marbling.

- Quality lamb should be pinkish red in color with a velvety texture and surrounded by a thin rim of brittle white fat. There should be little marbling.

## PURCHASING

Consider the cost per serving instead of the cost per pound when selecting a cut of meat. Bone and fat in a cut of meat can reduce the actual number of servings per pound of meat.

- Boneless meat: ¼ to ⅓ pound per serving (ground meat, meats for stews and soups, boneless roasts and steaks, liver and other variety meats).

- Bone-in meat: ⅓ to ½ pound per serving (roasts and steaks with moderate amount of bone).

- Bony meat: ¾ to 1 pound per serving (spareribs, short ribs, lamb riblets).

## REFRIGERATING AND FREEZING

Beef, veal, and lamb are perishable and must be wrapped properly, stored at a safe temperature, and used within a specified period of time. The cut of meat determines the length of time it may be refrigerated or frozen. Meat stored too long in the refrigerator will spoil. Meat kept in the freezer beyond the recommended period will lose flavor and become flabby as ice crystals formed by meat juices rupture the cells.

Fresh beef, veal, and lamb which are not to be frozen should be stored in the coldest part of the refrigerator or in the compartment designed for meat storage between 32° and 40° F.

Prepackaged beef, veal, and lamb may be stored, unopened, in the refrigerator in the original wrapping.

# CUTS OF VEAL

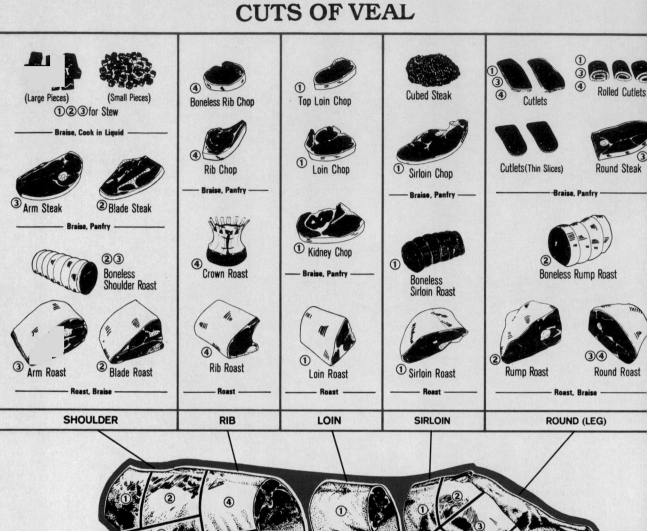

**SHOULDER**

(Large Pieces)    (Small Pieces)
① ② ③ for Stew

— Braise, Cook in Liquid —

③ Arm Steak    ② Blade Steak

— Braise, Panfry —

Boneless Shoulder Roast ② ③

③ Arm Roast    ② Blade Roast

— Roast, Braise —

**RIB**

④ Boneless Rib Chop

④ Rib Chop

— Braise, Panfry —

④ Crown Roast

④ Rib Roast

— Roast —

**LOIN**

① Top Loin Chop

① Loin Chop

① Kidney Chop

— Braise, Panfry —

① Loin Roast

— Roast —

**SIRLOIN**

Cubed Steak

① Sirloin Chop

— Braise, Panfry —

① Boneless Sirloin Roast

① Sirloin Roast

— Roast —

**ROUND (LEG)**

① ③ ④ Cutlets    ① ③ ④ Rolled Cutlets

Cutlets (Thin Slices)    ③ Round Steak

— Braise, Panfry —

② Boneless Rump Roast

② Rump Roast    ③ ④ Round Roast

— Roast, Braise —

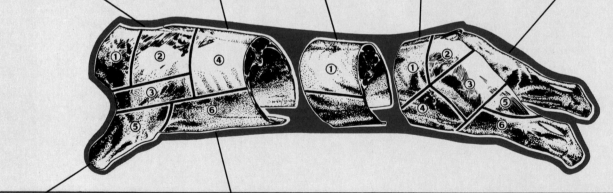

**SHANK**

⑤ Shank

⑤ Shank Cross Cuts

Braise, Cook in Liquid —

**BREAST**

⑥ Breast    ⑥ Stuffed Breast

— Roast, Braise —

⑥ Riblets    ⑥ Boneless Riblets    ⑥ Stuffed Chops

— Braise, Cook in Liquid —    — Braise, Panfry —

**VEAL FOR GRINDING OR CUBING**

Rolled Cubed Steaks    Ground Veal    Patties

— Braise —    — Roast (Bake) Braise, Panfry —

Mock Chicken Legs    City Chicken    Choplets

— Braise, Panfry —

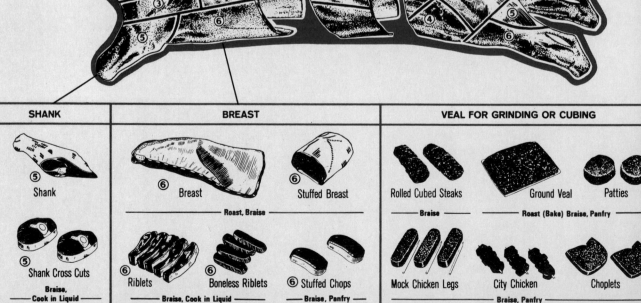

Prepackaged beef, veal, and lamb may be frozen without rewrapping for 1 to 2 weeks. For longer freezer storage, the original package should be overwrapped with special moisture-proof vapor-proof freezer wrapping material. Allow space around each package for good air circulation. Meat which has been frozen and thawed should be used immediately. Thawed meat should not be refrozen.

Cooked beef, veal, and lamb should be wrapped or covered and stored in the coldest part of the refrigerator within 1 to 2 hours after cooking. Covering the meat will prevent additional drying of the meat which has lost some moisture during cooking. Cooked meat will keep better and stay more moist if left in larger pieces and not cut until ready to use.

Fresh beef, veal, and lamb which have been frozen may be thawed in the refrigerator prior to cooking or during cooking. When thawing in the refrigerator, leave the meat in the original wrapper. If thawing during cooking, remove the wrapper and cook according to recipe directions.

## RECOMMENDED COOKING METHODS

Any beef, veal, or lamb cut of meat may be made tender, palatable, and flavorful if the appropriate cooking method is used. Tender cuts use dry heat methods while less tender cuts require cooking with moist heat.

### DRY HEAT

**Roasting:** To roast means to cook by dry heat in an oven without liquid. This is best for large tender cuts of meat.

Place the meat, fat side up, on a rack in a shallow roasting pan. The fat self-bastes the meat during cooking. Insert a meat thermometer so that the bulb rests in muscle tissue, not in fat or against bone. Do not cover. Cook until the meat reaches the desired degree of doneness or until the thermometer registers the recommended temperature.

**Broiling:** To broil means to cook by direct heat in an oven.

Set the oven on broil. Depending on the thickness of the cut, place the meat 2 to 5 inches

# RECOMMENDED STORAGE TIME FOR MEAT

| | Cut of Meat | Refrigeration Time (32°F - 40°F) | Freezer Time (0°F or lower) | Thawing Time in the Refrigerator |
|---|---|---|---|---|
| **BEEF** | Large Roast (6-8 pounds) | 2 to 4 days | 6 to 12 months | 4 to 7 hours per lb. |
| | Small Roast (4-5 pounds) | 2 to 4 days | 6 to 12 months | 3 to 5 hours per lb. |
| | Steak (1 inch thick) | 2 to 4 days | 6 to 12 months | 12 to 14 hours total |
| | Ground/Stew Meat | 1 to 2 days | 3 to 4 months | 8 to 12 hours total |
| | Leftover Cooked Beef | 4 to 5 days | 2 to 3 months | Varies |
| | Cured Beef | 6 to 7 days | Do not freeze | |
| **VEAL** | Roasts (4-5 pounds) | 5 to 6 days | 6 to 9 months | 3 to 5 hours per lb. |
| | Chops/Cutlets | 5 to 6 days | 6 to 9 months | 10 to 12 hours total |
| | Ground | 1 to 2 days | 3 to 4 months | 8 to 12 hours total |
| | Leftover Cooked Veal | 3 to 4 days | 2 to 3 months | Varies |
| **LAMB** | Large Roast (7-9 pounds) | 2 to 4 days | 6 to 9 months | 4 to 7 hours per lb. |
| | Small Roast (4-6 pounds) | 2 to 4 days | 6 to 9 months | 3 to 5 hours per lb. |
| | Chops/Steaks | 2 to 4 days | 6 to 9 months | 12 to 14 hours total |
| | Ground | 1 day | 3 to 4 months | 8 to 12 hours total |
| | Leftover Cooked Lamb | 4 to 5 days | 3 to 4 months | Varies |

# CUTS OF LAMB

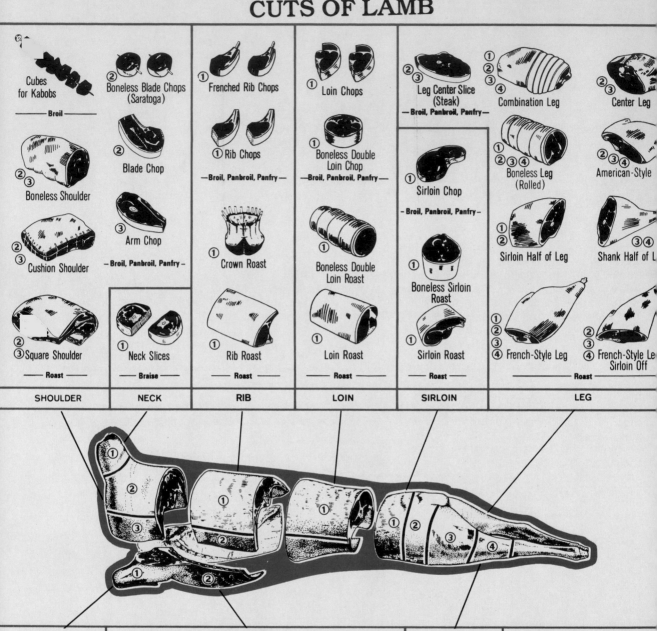

| SHOULDER | NECK | RIB | LOIN | SIRLOIN | LEG |
|---|---|---|---|---|---|

**SHOULDER**

Cubes for Kabobs — Broil

Boneless Blade Chops (Saratoga) ②

Blade Chop ②

Arm Chop ③
— Broil, Panbroil, Panfry —

Boneless Shoulder ②③

Cushion Shoulder ②③

Square Shoulder ②③ — Roast

**NECK**

Neck Slices ① — Braise

**RIB**

Frenched Rib Chops ①

Rib Chops ①
— Broil, Panbroil, Panfry —

Crown Roast ①

Rib Roast ① — Roast

**LOIN**

Loin Chops ①

Boneless Double Loin Chop ①
— Broil, Panbroil, Panfry —

Boneless Double Loin Roast ①

Loin Roast ① — Roast

**SIRLOIN**

Leg Center Slice (Steak) ①②③
— Broil, Panbroil, Panfry —

Sirloin Chop ①
— Broil, Panbroil, Panfry —

Boneless Sirloin Roast ①

Sirloin Roast ① — Roast

**LEG**

Combination Leg ①②③④

Center Leg ②③

Boneless Leg (Rolled) ①②③④

American-Style ②③④

Sirloin Half of Leg ①②

Shank Half of L ③④

French-Style Leg ①②③④

French-Style Le Sirloin Off ①②③④ — Roast

| FORE SHANK | BREAST | HIND SHANK | GROUND OR CUBED LAMB |
|---|---|---|---|

**FORE SHANK**

Fore Shank ①
— Braise, Cook in Liquid —

Riblets ②
— Braise, Cook in Liquid —

**BREAST**

Breast ②

Rolled Breast ②

Stuffed Breast ②
— Roast, Braise —

Boneless Riblets ②

Spareribs ②
— Braise, Roast (Bake) —

Stuffed Chops ②
— Broil, Panbroil, Panfry —

**HIND SHANK**

Hind Shank ④
— Braise, Cook in Liquid —

Cubed Steak
— Broil, Panbroil, Panfry —

**GROUND OR CUBED LAMB**

(Large Pieces)  Lamb for Stew  (Small P
— Braise, Cook in Liquid —

Lamb Patties

Ground Lamb
— Roast (Bake) —

© National Live Stock and Meat B

*Preparing for the judges' inspection at the Virginia State Fair, 1908.*

from the broiler element. Steaks and patties that are ¾ to 1 inch thick need to be 2 to 3 inches from the element; larger cuts from 1 to 2 inches thick should cook 3 to 5 inches from the heat source. Broil until the top browns; the meat should be about half-done at this point. Season with salt now. (Do not salt before cooking because salt draws out the moisture and inhibits browning of the meat.)

**Pan Broiling:** To pan broil is to cook by direct heat in a pan. This method is used for cooking the same cuts that may be broiled, but the cooking is done in a frying pan or griddle on top of the stove, not in the oven.

When pan broiling, do not add fat or water to the skillet unless the cut is extremely lean and a bit of fat is needed to prevent sticking. Cook slowly over medium low heat, turning occasionally to make sure that the meat browns evenly. Pour fat from pan as it accumulates.

**Frying:** Fried meats are cooked in oil over medium heat. For pan frying, use a small amount of oil; for deep fat frying, use enough oil to completely cover the meat. Pan frying is best for tender meat such as cubed beef steak that has been tenderized by pounding.

Heat oil over medium heat. When hot, add the meat and brown. Do not cover the skillet because the meat will lose its crispness. Continue to cook on medium heat until done, turning occasionally. Remove from pan and serve. During cooking, if the fat begins to smoke, lower the heat immediately.

### MOIST HEAT

**Braising:** Braised meats are cooked slowly in a small amount of liquid. The slow cooking and moisture from the liquid are vital for tenderizing tough cuts of meat.

Brown the meat in a small amount of fat; then pour off the pan drippings. The browning adds flavor and improves the appearance. Season the meat; add a small amount of liquid such as water, tomato juice, or soup. Cover tightly, and simmer until tender. Depending on the size of the cut, braising could take 1 to 4 hours. Make gravy with the pan drippings.

**Cooking in Liquid:** To cook in liquid, cover the meat completely with water or other liquid.

Brown the meat, cover with water, and add seasonings. Cover with a lid, and simmer gently until tender. Boiling tends to toughen the meat and increases shrinkage. If vegetables are to be cooked with the meat, add them near the end of the cooking time.

### USING A MEAT THERMOMETER

Many factors such as the temperature of the meat before it is cooked, its shape and thickness, and the fat and bone content determine the length of cooking time. It is difficult to visually judge the degree of doneness of meat. Therefore, for more accurate results, a meat thermometer is recommended.

Correct technique in using a meat thermometer is important. Insert the thermometer at an angle into the center of the meat so that the bulb of the thermometer rests in the center of the thickest part of the meat. Care should be taken to insure that the bulb is not touching bone or fat. The top of the thermometer should be as far away from the heat source as possible.

Meat continues to cook after it is removed from the heat source. It is important to remove the meat from the source of heat at a slightly lower degree of doneness than desired in the final product. The meat should be allowed to stand in a warm place for 15 minutes to complete the cooking process. Allowing the meat to stand will also make carving easier.

# ACKNOWLEDGMENTS

A Savory Lamb Pie, Maryland Baked Liver, Hannah Glasse's Veal Collops with Oyster Forcemeat, Marinated Veal Roast, Maryland Corned Beef Dinner, Planked Steak, Roast Beef with Yorkshire Pudding, Savory Rolled Roast of Veal, Veal Birds with Sour Cream, Veal Loin Chops with Asparagus adapted from *Maryland's Way* by Mrs. Lewis R. Andrews and Mrs. J. Reaney Kelly. By permission of the Hammond-Harwood House Association, Annapolis, Maryland.

Arkansas Pot Roast courtesy of Mrs. W.A. Rucker, Pine Bluff, Arkansas.

Bahama Kidneys in Red Wine, Greek Lamb with Zucchini, Picadillo adapted from *Jane Nickerson's Florida Cookbook*, ©1973. By permission of University Presses of Florida, Gainesville, Florida.

Baked Sesame Veal Cutlets, Beef Tenderloin with Bordelaise Sauce adapted from *The Gasparilla Cookbook*, compiled by The Junior League of Tampa, ©1961. By permission of The Junior League of Tampa, Florida.

Baked Veal with Noodles, Pineapple-Mint Lamb Ring adapted from *Collection of Rosamond Kershaw Seibels Recipes*. Printed by The R.L. Bryan Co., Columbia, South Carolina.

Barbecue Sauce, Steak à la Pitchfork adapted from *Dining with the Cattle Barons*, by Sarah Morgan, ©1981. Courtesy of Sarah Morgan, Ft. Worth, Texas.

Basic Brown Stock, Lamb Curry, Sautéed Liver with Avocado adapted from *The Jackson Cookbook*, ©1971. By permission of Symphony League of Jackson, Mississippi.

Beef and Pork Pasties, Beef Rouladen, Lucie County Beef Wellington adapted from *Indian River Cuisine*, ©1979. By permission of Indian River Community College Foundation, Fort Pierce, Florida.

Beef Hash with Indian Griddle Cakes, Pleasant Hill Round of Beef adapted from *Welcome Back to Pleasant Hill* by Elizabeth C. Kremer, ©1977. By permission of Shakertown at Pleasant Hill, Harrodsburg, Kentucky.

Beef Jerky, Breaded Sweetbreads, German Pot Roast and Vegetables, German Tongue with Raisin Sauce, Jardinière Sauce, Liver and Dumplings adapted from *Guten Appetit!*, compiled by the Sophienburg Museum, ©1978. By permission of Sophienburg Museum, New Braunfels, Texas.

Beef-Stuffed Green Peppers, Shakertown Meat Loaf adapted from *We Make You Kindly Welcome* by Elizabeth C. Kremer, ©1970. By permission of Shakertown at Pleasant Hill, Harrodsburg, Kentucky.

Blue Ribbon Round Steak adapted from *168 Prize Winning National Beef Cook-Off Recipes*, compiled by The American National CowBelles.

Broiled Steak with Mushroom-Wine Sauce, Carpetbag Steak, Salzburger Sauerbraten, Mushroom Pan Gravy, Sweet-and-Sour Tomato Sauce adapted from *Savannah Sampler Cookbook* by Margaret Wayt DeBolt, ©1978. By permission of The Donning Company/Publishers, Inc., Norfolk, Virginia.

Cajun Special adapted from *Acadiana Profile's Cajun Cooking*, edited by Trent Angers and Sue McDonough. By permission of Angers Publishing Corp., Lafayette, Louisiana.

Country Beef Sausage adapted from *Pioneer Cookery Around Oklahoma*, compiled and edited by Linda Kennedy Rosser, ©1978. By permission of Bobwhite Publications, Oklahoma City, Oklahoma.

Creole Beef, Crown Roast of Lamb with Fruit Dressing, Veal Lorraine adapted from *Plantation Cookbook* by The Junior League of New Orleans. By permission of Doubleday, Inc., New York.

Daube Glacé, Rolled Meat Loaf with Walnuts and Oranges, Stuffed Veal Roast, Virginia Spiced Beef Round adapted from *Marion Brown's Southern Cook Book*, ©1951. By permission of University of North Carolina Press, Chapel Hill, North Carolina.

Garlic Roasted Leg of Lamb, Horseradish-Mustard Sauce prepared for photography by Mrs. Sallie Warner, Nashville, Tennessee.

Georgia Tearoom Swiss Steak adapted from *The Frances Virginia Tea Room Cookbook* by Mildred Huff Coleman, ©1981. By permission of Peachtree Publishers Limited, Atlanta.

German Steak Rolls, German-Style Meatballs, Texas Prize Brisket of Beef adapted from *Square House Museum Cookbook*. By permission of Carson County Square House Museum, Panhandle, Texas.

Greek-Stuffed Beef Rolls, Mrs. Lyndon B. Johnson's Fillet of Beef, Shish Kabobs, Stuffed Veal Roast with Dauphine Potatoes adapted from *Come Cook With Us: A Treasury of Greek Cooking* by The Hellenic Woman's Club, ©1967. By permission of The Hellenic Woman's Club, Norfolk, Virginia.

Greenbrier Roast Sirloin of Beef, Veal Scallopini Maryland adapted from *Legendary Specialties From The Greenbrier*. Courtesy of The Greenbrier, White Sulphur Springs, West Virginia.

Henry Bane Steak Sauce, Johnnie Marzetti, Old-Fashioned Chopped Southern Beef Hash, Veal Chops in Casserole adapted from *Out of Kentucky Kitchens* by Marion Flexner, ©1949. By permission of Franklin Watts, Inc., New York.

Hot Tamale Pie adapted from *Gourmet of the Delta* by The Episcopal Women of St. John's Mission, Leland, Mississippi, and St. Paul's Church, Hollandale, Mississippi.

Hot Tamales courtesy of Mrs. H.J. Sherrer, Bay City, Texas.

Hotel Roanoke Steak Diane, Hotel Roanoke Veal Piccata, Rack of Lamb adapted from *Hotel Roanoke Most Requested Recipes*. Courtesy of Hotel Roanoke, Roanoke, Virginia.

Kentucky Round Steak adapted from *Famous Kentucky Recipes*, compiled by Cabbage Patch Circle, Louisville, Kentucky.

Lamb Pilaf, Lamb Shanks Baked in Fruited Wine, Sweet-and-Sour Brisket with Sauerkraut adapted from *Good Cooks Never Lack Friends* by Sisterhood Agudath Achim Synagogue, ©1978. By permission of Sisterhood of Congregation Agudath Achim, Savannah, Georgia.

Liver Nips adapted from *Talk About Good!*, compiled by The Junior League of Lafayette, Inc., ©1969. By permission of The Junior League of Lafayette, Inc., Lafayette, Louisiana.

Mexican Steak adapted from *It Seems Like I Done it This-'A-Way* by Cleo Stiles Bryan, ©1980. By permission of Cleo Stiles Bryan, Tahlequah, Oklahoma.

1944 Crustless Lamb Pie, Wartime Lamb Pie adapted from *Forgotten Recipes*, compiled and updated by Jaine Rodack, ©1981. By permission of Wimmer Bros. Books, Memphis, Tennessee.

Original Texas-Style Bowl of Red, Pedernales River Chili adapted from *A Bowl of Red* by Frank X. Tolbert, ©1972. By permission of Doubleday, Inc., New York.

Panhandle Barbecue Sauce courtesy of Marian Williams, Bartlesville, Oklahoma.

Pastitsio, Welsh Meat Loaf adapted from *Georgia Heritage - Treasured Recipes*, ©1979. By permission of The National Society of The Colonial Dames of America in the State of Georgia, Huntsville, Georgia.

Polish Meat Pies adapted from *The Saga of Texas Cookery* by Sarah Morgan. Courtesy of Sarah Morgan, Ft. Worth, Texas.

Roast Lamb with Anchovies adapted from *Charleston Receipts*, collected by The Junior League of Charleston, ©1950. By permission of The Junior League of Charleston, South Carolina.

Slumgullion, Steak Birds, Veal Fricassee, Veal Oysters adapted from *Recipes From Old Virginia*, compiled by The Virginia Federation of Home Demonstration Clubs, ©1958. By permission of The Virginia Extension Homemakers Council, Austinville, Virginia.

Son-of-a-Gun Stew adapted from *Chuckwagon Cooking* by Jalyn Burkett. By permission of Texas Agricultural Extension Service and Texas A&M University System, Ft. Worth, Texas.

Steak and Kidney Pudding adapted from *The Melting Pot: Ethnic Cuisine in Texas* by The Institute of Texan Cultures, ©1977. By permission of The University of Texas Institute of Texan Cultures, San Antonio, Texas.

Tennessee Spiced Round of Beef adapted from *The Nashville Cookbook* by Nashville Area Home Economics Association, Nashville, Tennessee. Spiced round courtesy of Baltz Brothers Packing Company, Nashville, Tennessee.

Tennessee Spiced Round of Beef prepared for photography by Mrs. Elizabeth Dennis, Nashville, Tennessee.

Tony's Italian Pasta-Meat Pie, Veal Scallopini courtesy of Anthony Cannerella Mathews, Savannah, Georgia.

Veal Birds adapted from *The James K. Polk Cookbook*, compiled by The James K. Polk Memorial Auxiliary, ©1978. By permission of The James K. Polk Memorial Auxiliary, Columbia, Tennessee.

Veal Curry adapted from *Virginia Cookery - Past and Present* by The Woman's Auxiliary of Olivet Episcopal Church, Franconia, Virginia.

Veal Cutlets Provençal adapted from *Recipes From The Old South* by Martha Meade ©1961. By permission of Holt, Rinehart and Winston, New York.

Veal in Paprika Cream adapted from *The Gardener's Cook Book*, edited by Mildred W. Schlumpf. Published by The Houston Council of Texas Garden Clubs, Inc.

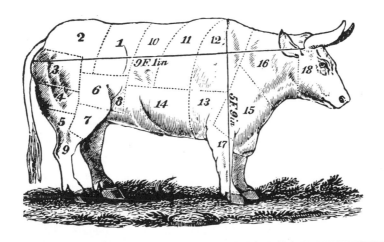

# INDEX

Anchovies, Roast Lamb with, 88
Appetizers
  Beef Empanadas, 47
  Liver Nips, 114
  Sweetbreads Wrapped in
    Bacon, 115
Asparagus, Veal Loin Chops
  with, 67
Avocado
  Guacamole, 37
  Liver with Avocado, Sautéed, 110

Barbecue
  Brisket, Grilled, 16
  Brisket of Beef, Barbecued, 16
  Brisket, Oven-Barbecued, 16
  Lamb, Oven-Barbecued, 87
  Lamb Shanks, Barbecued, 97
  Roast, Oven-Barbecued, 19
  Sauce, Barbecue, 16, 126
  Sauce, Creole Barbecue, 127
  Sauce, LBJ's Barbecue, 127
  Sauce, Panhandle Barbecue, 16
Beans
  Pinto Beans, 51
  Red Beans and Hamburger, 42
BEEF
  Bourguignon, Bœuf, 36
  Bowl of Red, Original
    Texas-Style, 53
  Brisket
    Barbecued Brisket of Beef, 16
    Corned Beef, 22
    Corned Beef Dinner,
      Maryland, 23
    Grilled Brisket, 16
    Oven-Barbecued Brisket, 16
    Stew, Brisket, 54
    Sweet-and-Sour Brisket with
      Sauerkraut, 17
    Texas Prize Brisket of Beef, 17
  Chili, Alabama, 51
  Chili, Pedernales River, 51
  Chipped Beef on Toast, 25
  Corned Beef, 22
  Corned Beef Dinner,
    Maryland, 23
  German Steak Rolls, 36
  Greek-Stuffed Beef Rolls, 35
  Hash, Old-Fashioned Chopped
    Southern Beef, 55
  Hash with Indian Griddle Cakes,
    Beef, 56
  Jerky, Beef, 25

Loaf of Beef, Jellied, 57
Pie, Beef Pot, 56
Pie, Deep-Dish Beef, 55
Ragôut, Beef, 54
Roasts
  Beef à la Mode, 20
  Beef Tenderloin with
    Bordelaise Sauce, 10
  Beef Wellington, Lucie
    County, 12
  Daube Roast, 21
  Fillet of Beef, Mrs. Lyndon B.
    Johnson's, 11
  Fillet of Beef, Turn-of-the
    Century, 11
  Oven-Barbecued Roast, 19
  Pot Roast and Vegetables,
    German, 21
  Pot Roast, Arkansas, 19
  Pot Roast, Chuck Wagon, 18
  Pot Roast, Creole, 20
  Pot Roast, Stove-Top, 21
  Pot Roast, Sunday Dinner, 19
  Prime Rib of Beef, North
    Carolina, 12
  Rib Roast, Bourbon, 14
  Rib Roast, Standing, 12
  Round of Beef, Pleasant
    Hill, 21
  Sauerbraten, Quick, 23
  Sauerbraten, Salzburger, 23
  Sirloin of Beef, Greenbrier
    Roast, 14
  Stew from Sunday's Roast, 55
  Yorkshire Pudding, Roast Beef
    with, 14
Rolls, Roast Beef, 57
Rouladen, Beef, 35
Sauerbraten, Quick, 23
Sauerbraten, Salzburger, 23
Slumgullion, 57
Spiced Beef Round, Virginia, 25
Spiced Round of Beef,
  Tennessee, 25
Steaks
  à la Pitchfork, Steak, 26
  Birds, Steak, 34
  Bourguignon, Bœuf, 36
  Broiled Steak with
    Mushroom-Wine Sauce, 27
  Carpetbag Steak, 29
  Chicken-Fried Steak, 30
  Country-Fried Steak, On The
    Trail, 31

Cubed Steak with Onion, 31
Diane, Hotel Roanoke
  Steak, 27
Fajitas, 37
Filet Mignon, Pan-Broiled, 27
Fingers, Steak, 32
Flank Steak, New Orleans, 30
Flank Steak, Oklahoma, 29
Mexican Steak, 36
Planked Steak, 26
Pudding, Steak and
  Kidney, 109
Roll, Fruited Steak, 29
Rolls, German Steak, 36
Rolls, Greek-Stuffed Beef, 35
Rouladen, Beef, 35
Round Steak, Blue Ribbon, 34
Round Steak, Kentucky, 33
Spanish Steak, 27
Stroganoff, Beef, 36
Swiss Steak, Georgia
  Tearoom, 32
Texas Steak, 26
Stew, Brisket, 54
Stew from Sunday's Roast, 55
Stew, Old-Fashioned Beef, 54
Beef, Ground
  Cajun Special, 41
  Cheeseburgers, Grilled, 40
  Chili, Pedernales River, 51
  Creole Beef, 42
  Empanadas, Beef, 47
  Enchiladas, Texas, 48
  Filet Mignon, Mock, 41
  Green Peppers, Beef-Stuffed, 50
  Hamburger, Red Beans and, 42
  Hamburger Steak Deluxe, 40
  Hash, Texas Ground Beef, 42
  Hot Tamales, 48
  Johnnie Marzetti, 43
  Meatballs, German-Style, 39
  Meat Loaf, Shakertown, 39
  Meat Loaf, Welsh, 39
  Meat Loaf with Walnuts and
    Oranges, Rolled, 38
  Pasties, Beef and Pork, 45
  Picadillo, 42
  Pie, Hot Tamale, 46
  Pie, Louisiana Meat, 45
  Pie, Tony's Italian
    Pasta-Meat, 43
  Pies, Polish Meat, 46
  Porcupines, Beef, 39
  Rolls, Stuffed Cabbage, 50

Beef, Ground (continued)
  Sausage, Country Beef, 50
  Steaks, Mock Chicken-Fried, 41
  Tacos, 48
Biscuits, Baking Powder, 110
Bordelaise Sauce, 10, 125
Bourguignon, Bœuf, 36
Brains
  Sherry Sauce, Brains in, 108
  Stew, Son-of-a-Gun, 120
Breads
  Baking Powder Biscuits, 110
  Farina Balls, 101
  Griddle Cakes, Indian, 56
  Yorkshire Puddings,
    Individual, 14
Butter
  Maître d'Hôtel Butter, 29
  Sauce, au Beurre Noir, 124
  Steak Butter, 126

Cabbage Rolls, Stuffed, 50
Cajun Special, 41
Casseroles
  Johnnie Marzetti, 43
  Pastitsio, 104
  Slumgullion, 57
  Veal Chops in Casserole, 67
Cheeseburgers, Grilled, 40
Chicken-Fried Steak, 30
Chicken-Fried Steaks, Mock, 41
Chili
  Alabama Chili, 51
  Bowl of Red, Original
    Texas-Style, 53
  Pedernales River Chili, 51
Chive Sauce, Sour Cream
  and, 127
Cooking Methods,
  Recommended, 135
Cranberry Glaze, 90
Creole
  Barbecue Sauce, Creole, 127
  Beef, Creole, 42
  Lamb Stew, Creole, 99
  Pot Roast, Creole, 20
  Sauce, Baked Liver in
    Creole, 113
Croquettes, Veal, 80
Curry
  Lamb Curry, 105
  Veal Curry, 77
Cuts of Beef, 132
Cuts of Lamb, 136
Cuts of Veal, 134

Daube Glacé, 65
Dressings. See Stuffings.
Dumplings
  Liver and Dumplings, 114
  Veal Pot Roast with
    Dumplings, 65

Enchiladas, Texas, 48

Fajitas, 37
Farina Balls, 101
Filet Mignon, Mock, 41
Filet Mignon, Pan-Broiled, 27

Filling, Mushroom Pâté, 12
Fricassee, Veal, 78
Fruit
  Avocado, Sautéed Liver
    with, 110
  Cranberry Glaze, 90
  Dressing, Fruit, 85
  Oranges, Rolled Meat Loaf with
    Walnuts and, 38
  Pineapple, Lena's Lamb Chops
    and, 96
  Pineapple-Mint Lamb Ring, 105
  Plum Sauce, Leg of Lamb
    with, 90
  Raisin Sauce, German Tongue
    with, 120
  Sauce, Spicy Fruit, 129
  Steak Roll, Fruited, 29
  Wine, Lamb Shanks Baked in
    Fruited, 97

German Pot Roast and
  Vegetables, 21
German Steak Rolls, 36
Glaze, 85, 92
Glaze, Cranberry, 90
Gravies. See also Sauces.
  Brown Gravy, 63
  Cream Gravy, 131
  Mushroom Pan Gravy, 131
  Roast Pan Gravy, 131
  Tomato Gravy, 103
Greek-Stuffed Beef Rolls, 35
Greek Lamb with Zucchini, 98
Griddle Cakes, Indian, 56
Guacamole, 37

Hash
  Beef Hash, Old-Fashioned
    Chopped Southern, 55
  Beef Hash with Indian Griddle
    Cakes, 56
  Ground Beef Hash, Texas, 42
  Lamb Hash, 104
Horseradish
  Sauce, Horseradish, 17, 21, 128
  Sauce, Horseradish and Sour
    Cream, 128
  Sauce, Horseradish-
    Mustard, 128

Jellied Loaf of Beef, 57
Jelly, Jalapeño, 130
Jerky, Beef, 25
Johnnie Marzetti, 43

Kidney
  Pie, Kidney, 110
  Pudding, Steak and Kidney, 109
  Red Wine, Bahama Kidneys
    in, 108
  Stew, Son-of-a-Gun, 120

Lamb
  Chops
    Baked Lamb Chops, 96
    Breaded Lamb Chops, 95
    Broiled Lamb Riblets, 94
    Grilled Lamb Chops, 94

Pineapple, Lena's Lamb Chops
    and, 96
  Planked Lamb Chops, 95
  Sautéed Lamb Chops, 95
Crown Roast of Lamb with Fruit
  Dressing, 85
Curry, Lamb, 105
Hash, Lamb, 104
Leg of Lamb
  à la Bérnaise, Lamb Roast, 90
  Anchovies, Roast Lamb
    with, 88
  Braised Leg of Lamb, Troth's
    Fortune, 89
  Glazed Leg of Lamb, 90
  Glazed Stuffed Lamb, 92
  Grilled Lamb, 86
  Herbed Roast Lamb, 88
  Oven-Barbecued Lamb, 87
  Lemon Garlic Leg of Lamb, 86
  Plum Sauce, Leg of Lamb
    with, 90
  Stuffed Leg of Lamb, 92
Pastitsio, 104
Patties with Tomato Gravy,
  Lamb, 103
Pie, A Savory Lamb, 103
Pie, 1944 Crustless Lamb, 101
Pie, Shepherd's, 103
Pie, Wartime Lamb, 102
Pilaf, Lamb, 99
Ragôut of Lamb, 101
Riblets, Broiled Lamb, 94
Ring, Pineapple-Mint
  Lamb, 105
Ring, Springtime Lamb, 104
Roasts. See also Leg of Lamb.
  Crown Roast of Lamb with
    Fruit Dressing, 85
  Rack of Lamb, 84
  Pot Roast, Lamb, 93
  Shoulder, Roasted Lamb, 93
  Saddle of Lamb, 84
Shanks Baked in Fruited Wine,
  Lamb, 97
Shanks, Barbecued Lamb, 97
Shanks, Braised Lamb, 97
Shish Kabobs, 98
Stew, Creole Lamb, 99
Stew, Indian, 100
Stew, Lamb, 99
Stew, Navajo, 100
Zucchini, Greek Lamb with, 98
Liver
  Baked Liver in Creole
    Sauce, 113
  Baked Liver, Maryland, 112
  Dumplings, Liver and, 114
  Grilled Calves' Liver, 112
  Nips, Liver, 114
  Sautéed Liver with
    Avocado, 110
  Smothered Liver and
    Onions, 110
  Sour Cream, Calves' Liver
    in, 112
  Stew, Son-of-a-Gun, 120
Mexican Sauce, 129
Mexican Steak, 36

Mint
  Lamb Ring, Pineapple-Mint, 105
  Pastry Shell, Mint, 102
  Sauce, Mint, 129
  Sauce, Tangy Mint, 130
Mushrooms
  Filling, Mushroom Pâté, 12
  Gravy, Mushroom Pan, 131
  Sauce, Broiled Steak with
    Mushroom-Wine, 27
  Sauce, Mushroom, 126
  Sauce, Sherry-Mushroom, 11
  Veal Chops with Mushrooms, 69
  Veal Collops with Oyster
    Forcemeat, Hannah
    Glasse's, 76

Noodles
  Beef Stroganoff, 36
  Johnnie Marzetti, 43
  Meatballs, German-Style, 39
  Veal and Noodle Stew, 78
  Veal Chop Delight, 67
  Veal in Paprika Cream, 78
  Veal Meatballs, 80
  Veal with Noodles, Baked, 77

Onions
  Cubed Steak with Onion, 31
  Smothered Liver and
    Onions, 110
Oysters
  Carpetbag Steak, 29
  Sweetbread and Oyster Pie, 118
  Veal Collops with Oyster
    Forcemeat, Hannah
    Glasse's, 76
  Veal Oysters, 78

Pastitsio, 104
Pâté Filling, Mushroom, 12
Peppers
  Bowl of Red, Original
    Texas-Style, 53
  Green Peppers, Beef-Stuffed, 50
  Jalapeño Jelly, 130
  Pico de Gallo, 37
Picadillo, 42
Pies and Pastries
  Beef and Pork Pasties, 45
  Beef Pot Pie, 56
  Beef Pie, Deep-Dish, 55
  Empanadas, Beef, 47
  Hot Tamale Pie, 46
  Kidney Pie, 110
  Lamb Pie, A Savory, 103
  Lamb Pie, 1944 Crustless, 101
  Lamb Pie, Wartime, 102
  Meat Pie, Louisiana, 45
  Meat Pie, Tony's Italian
    Pasta-, 43
  Meat Pies, Polish, 46
  Mint Pastry Shell, 102
  Pastry, 12
  Shepherd's Pie, 103
  Suet Crust, 109
  Sweetbread and Oyster Pie, 118
  Sweetbreads in Pastry Shells,
    Sherried, 118
  Sweet Potato Pastry, 47

Pineapple
  Pineapple, Lena's Lamb Chops
    and, 96
  Pineapple-Mint Lamb Ring, 105
Pork
  Meatballs, German-Style, 39
  Pasties, Beef and Pork, 45
  Veal Birds, 74
  Veal Loaf, 79
Potatoes
  Dauphine Potatoes, 64
  Hash, Old-Fashioned Chopped
    Southern Beef, 55
  New Potatoes, Oven-Roasted Veal
    with, 60
  Pastry, Sweet Potato, 47
  Planked Steak, 26
  Shepherd's Pie, 103
  Swiss Steak, Georgia
    Tearoom, 32
Puddings
  Steak and Kidney Pudding, 109
  Yorkshire Puddings,
    Individual, 14
Purchasing, 133

Ragôut
  Beef Ragôut, 54
  Ragôut of Lamb, 101
Recommended Storage Time for
  Meat, 135
Refrigerating and Freezing, 133
Relish, Piquant, 129
Rice
  Beef Porcupines, 39
  Beef-Stuffed Green Peppers, 50
  Cajun Special, 41
  Creole Beef, 42
  Creole Pot Roast, 20
  Grillades Louisiane, 69
  Lamb Curry, 105
  Lamb Pilaf, 99
  Picadillo, 42
  Stuffing, Veal Roast with
    Rice, 62
  Veal Curry, 77
Rouladen, Beef, 35

Sauces. See also Gravies.
  au Beurre Noir, Sauce, 124
  Barbecue Sauce, 16, 126
  Barbecue Sauce, Creole, 127
  Barbecue Sauce, LBJ's, 127
  Barbecue Sauce, Panhandle, 16
  Basting Sauce, 14
  Béarnaise, Sauce, 124
  Béchamel, Sauce, 124
  Bordelaise Sauce, 10, 125
  Brown Sauce, Basic, 125
  Butter, Maître d'Hôtel, 29
  Fruit Sauce, Spicy, 129
  Horseradish and Sour Cream
    Sauce, 128
  Horseradish-Mustard
    Sauce, 128
  Horseradish Sauce, 17, 21, 128
  Hot Sauce, 48
  Jardinière Sauce, 126
  Madeira Sauce, 125

  Marinade Sauce, Tangy, 127
  Mexican Sauce, 129
  Mint Sauce, 129
  Mint Sauce, Tangy, 130
  Mushroom Sauce, 126
  Pico de Gallo, 37
  Sherry-Mushroom Sauce, 11
  Sour Cream and Chive
    Sauce, 127
  Sour Cream Sauce, 46
  Spanish Sauce, 129
  Steak Sauce, Henry Bane, 127
  Tomato Sauce, 128
  Tomato Sauce,
    Sweet-and-Sour, 129
  Wine Sauce, Spiced Port, 130
Sauerbraten, Salzburger, 23
Sauerkraut, Sweet-and-Sour
  Brisket with, 17
Sausage
  Hot Tamales, 48
  Pasta-Meat Pie, Tony's
    Italian, 43
  Sausage, Country Beef, 50
  Veal Birds, 74
Selecting Quality Meat, 133
Shepherd's Pie, 103
Shish Kabobs, 98
Slumgullion, 57
Son-of-a-Gun Stew, 120
Soufflé, Veal, 81
Soups and Stews
  Beef Stew, Old-Fashioned, 54
  Bowl of Red, Original
    Texas-Style, 53
  Brisket Stew, 54
  Indian Stew, 100
  Lamb Stew, 99
  Lamb Stew, Creole, 99
  Navajo Stew, 100
  Ragôut, Beef, 54
  Ragôut of Lamb, 101
  Roast, Stew from Sunday's, 55
  Son-of-a-Gun Stew, 120
  Veal and Noodle Stew, 78
  Veal Stew, 79
Sour Cream
  Calves' Liver in Sour Cream, 112
  Sauce, Horseradish and Sour
    Cream, 128
  Sauce, Sour Cream, 46
  Sauce, Sour Cream and
    Chive, 127
  Veal and Noodle Stew, 78
  Veal Birds with Sour Cream, 75
  Veal Meatballs, 80
Stock, Basic Brown, 125
Stroganoff, Beef, 36
Stuffings and Dressings
  Dressing, 63
  Fruit Dressing, 85
  Rice Stuffing, 62
  Stuffing, 38
Sweet-and-Sour
  Brisket with Sauerkraut,
    Sweet-and-Sour, 17
  Sauce, Sweet-and-Sour
    Tomato, 129
  Tongue, Sweet-and-Sour, 119

Sweetbreads
  Bacon, Sweetbreads Wrapped
    in, 115
  Breaded Sweetbreads, 116
  Broiled Sweetbreads with Lemon
    Sauce, 115
  Deluxe, Sweetbreads, 116
  Pie, Sweetbread and Oyster, 118
  Sautéed Sweetbreads with
    Gravy, 116
  Sherried Sweetbreads in Pastry
    Shells, 118
  Stew, Son-of-a-Gun, 120
Suet Crust, 109
Sweet Potato Pastry, 47

Tacos, 48
Tamales
  Pie, Hot Tamale, 46
  Tamales, Hot, 48
Thermometer, Using a Meat, 137
Tomatoes
  Beef Empanadas, 47
  Gravy, Tomato, 103
  Sauce, Sweet-and-Sour
    Tomato, 129
  Sauce, Tomato, 128
Tongue
  Pickled Tongue, 119
  Raisin Sauce, German Tongue
    with, 120
  Sweet-and-Sour Tongue, 119
Tripe, Breaded, 120

Using a Meat Thermometer, 137

Veal
  Baked Veal with Noodles, 77
  Birds, Veal, 74
  Birds with Sour Cream,
    Veal, 75
  Brains in Sherry Sauce. 108

Chops
  Asparagus, Veal Loin Chops
    with, 67
  Baked Veal Chops, 66
  Breaded Veal Chops, 66
  Casserole, Veal Chops in, 67
  Cream Sauce, Veal Chops in, 67
  Lorraine, Veal, 68
  Mushrooms, Veal Chops
    with, 69
Croquettes, Veal, 80
Curry, Veal, 77
Cutlets
  Baked Sesame Veal Cutlets, 74
  Birds, Veal, 74
  Birds with Sour Cream,
    Veal, 75
  Collops with Oyster Forcemeat,
    Hannah Glasse's Veal, 76
  Grillades Louisiane, 69
  Grillades Panée, 69
  Marsala, Veal, 70
  Paprika Veal, 70
  Parmigiana, Veal, 70
  Piccata, Hotel Roanoke
    Veal, 71
  Provençal, Veal Cutlets, 73
  Scallopini Maryland, Veal, 73
  Scallopini, Veal, 73
  Wiener Schnitzel, 74
Fricassee, Veal, 78
Grillades Louisiane, 69
Grillades Panée, 69
Loaf, Veal, 79
Lorraine, Veal, 68
Meatballs, Veal, 80
Oysters, Veal, 78
Paprika Cream, Veal in, 78
Roasts
  Daube Glacé, 65
  Marinated Veal Roast, 60
  Oven-Roasted Veal with New
    Potatoes, 60

Pot Roast, Veal, 65
Pot Roast with Dumplings,
  Veal, 65
Rice Stuffing, Veal Roast
  with, 62
Rolled Roast of Veal,
  Savory, 60
Rolled Veal Roast,
  Louisiana, 62
Stuffed Veal Roast, 63
Stuffed Veal Roast with
  Dauphine Potatoes, 64
Soufflé, Veal, 81
Stew, Son-of-a-Gun, 120
Stew, Veal, 79
Stew, Veal and Noodle, 78
Woodstock, 81
Vegetables
  Asparagus, Veal Loin Chops
    with, 67
  Cabbage Rolls, Stuffed, 50
  Dauphine Potatoes, Stuffed Veal
    Roast with, 64
  Green Peppers, Beef-Stuffed, 50
  Mushrooms, Veal Chops
    with, 69
  New Potatoes, Oven-Roasted Veal
    with, 60
  Onions, Smothered Liver
    and, 110
  Pot Roast and Vegetables,
    German, 21
  Sweet Potato Pastry, 47
  Zucchini, Greek Lamb with, 98

Walnuts and Oranges, Rolled
  Meat Loaf with, 38
Wiener Schnitzel, 74
Woodstock, 81

Zucchini, Greek Lamb with, 98

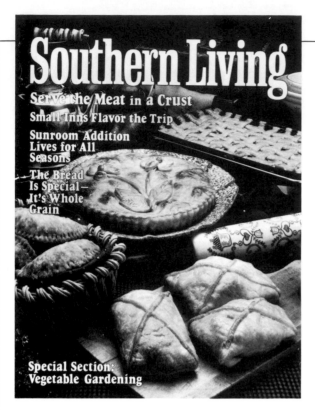